The Royal Dragoon Guards formed in 1992 as a result of an amalgamation of the 4/7th Royal Dragoon Guards and the 5th Inniskilling Dragoon Guards. It is they who carry the burden of maintaining the traditions and honours of the parent regiments. The 4th Royal Irish Dragoon Guards, the 5th Dragoon Guards (PCW), the 6th Inniskilling Dragoons and the 7th (Princess Royals) Dragoon Guards. There are Battle Honours on the Regimental Standard, bearing evidence of 225 years of past battles. Korea and the Hook were added after the 1950-53 Korean War. The Regiment has already experienced the wars in Iraq and Afghanistan. By co-ordinating personal accounts and other records this book will assist future historians to update that history and serve as a permanent record of those who paid the price with their lives.

In the Summer the paddy fields were nearly impassable to tanks. Tank Commanders and drivers had to display great skill. Room for manouvre in the valleys was limited.

A Track in Korea.

# Tracks in Korea

## (An Anthology)

Captain C.J.Boardman

First published by Dragoon Publications 2013

© Captain C.J. Boardman 2013

All rights reserved. No part of this book may be reprinted or reproduced or utlilised in any form or by any electronic, mechanical, or other means, now known or hereafter invented, including photocopying and recording, or in any information storage or retrieval system, without permission in writing from the publisher

ISBN: 978-0-9927780-0-2

Produced by Shore Books and Design
Blackborough End, King's Lynn, Norfolk PE32 1SF

# CONTENTS

| | |
|---|---|
| ABBREVIATIONS | vii |
| FOREWORD | ix |
| FARE THEE WELL INNISKILLING | 1 |
| ACKNOWLEDGEMENTS OF COPYRIGHTS | 5 |
| UN FORCES CONTRIBUTION | 8 |
| CASUALTIES | 11 |
| PROGRESSION TO CONFLICT | 13 |
| THE NORTH KOREAN INVASION | 15 |
| ENTER THE CHINESE | 19 |
| THE IMJIN BATTLE | 29 |
| THE 8TH KINGS ROYAL IRISH HUSSARS | 50 |
| CITATION | 56 |
| PREPARATION, A CALL TO ARM OURSELVES | 57 |
| THE VOYAGE | 68 |
| INTO BATTLE | 76 |
| POEM BY Cft. D.A. PEARSON | 99 |
| OPERATIONS LIVERPOOL, JEHU AND ASCOT | 104 |
| A STUFFED FISH IN A GLASS CASE | 121 |
| NEWSLETTERS | 130 |
| THE REGIMENTAL SIGNAL SERGEANTS RECALL, by Sgt Derek Wetmore | 135 |
| A NAVAL VENTURE BY MAJOR GENERAL H.G. WOODS CB, MBE, MC,DL,DLiTT | 138 |
| AN EARLY FLIGHT | 141 |
| THE HOOK BY COLONEL MJ ANSTICE MC | 151 |
| REST AND RECUPERATION | 162 |
| A MOMENT OF GLORY WHICH FAILED | 168 |

| | |
|---|---|
| AN INFANTRY PATROL | 171 |
| PROPAGANDA | 176 |
| THE PRICE OF PEACE, A TRIBUTE TO HARRY COOKSON | 184 |
| SUMMING UP | 188 |
| A RAT STORY BY DON POOLEY | 190 |
| A SAD FAREWELL | 194 |
| THE FINAL DAYS | 203 |
| LAST THOUGHTS BY MAJOR GENERAL H.G. WOODS CB, MBE,MC,DL,DLiTT | 208 |
| HONOURS AND AWARDS | 210 |
| ROLL OF HONOUR | 212 |
| A LETTER OF THANKS FROM THE PRESIDENT OF KOREA | 214 |
| VETERANS AT WESTMINSTER ABBEY 2013 | Back Cover |

# ABREVIATION AND EXPLANATIONS

| | |
|---|---|
| ARV | Armoured Recovery Vehicle |
| DRAC | Directorate Royal Armoured Corp |
| FOO | Forward Observation Officer |
| FDLs | Forward Defended Lines |
| HE | High Explosive |
| HAD | Heavy Aid Detachment (REME) |
| LAD | Light Aid Detachment (REME) |
| RHQ | Regimental Headquarter |

Neutral Turn – A tank is able to turn on its axis by operating the two tracks in opposite directions at the same time.

| | |
|---|---|
| SP | Support Vehicle |
| UN | United Nations |

## RANKS

| | |
|---|---|
| CO | Commanding Officer |
| RSM | Regimental Sergeant Major |
| CSM | Company Sergeant Major |
| RQMS | Regimental Quarter Master Sergeant |
| SSM | Squadron Sergeant Major |
| TQMS | Technical Quartermaster Sergeant |
| SQMS | Squadron Quartermaster Sergeant |
| SGT | Sergeant |
| CPL | Corporal |
| LCPL | Lance Corporal |
| TPR | Trooper |
| Cfn | Craftsman |

| | |
|---|---|
| NCO | Non-commissioned Officer, i.e. - Lance Corporals to Sergeants |
| WO | Warrant Officer |

## DECORATIONS

| | |
|---|---|
| VC | Victoria Cross |
| DSO | Distinguished Service Order |
| MC | Military Cross |
| MM | Military Medal |
| MID | Mentioned in Dispatches |

# FOREWORD

By Major General Henry Woods CB, MBE, MC, DL.
(Formerly Chairman 5th Royal Inniskilling Dragoon Guards Association)

It is a great privilege to be associated with this work of remembering sacrifices and service. 2012 marked the 60th anniversary of the year that the 5th Royal Inniskilling Dragoon Guards spent in Korea as the UK Armoured Regiment in the 1st Commonwealth Division, under United Nations Command. The peak of fierce fighting had already passed when the Regiment took over from the 8th Kings' Royal Irish Hussars in December 1951. The seemingly endless Armistice Talks at Panmunjom moved slowly towards a truce. Meanwhile desultory and occasionally prolonged exchanges of fire and spoiling attacks imposed on both sides vigilance, thorough planning (counter-attacks and Defensive Fire tasks) as well as a persistent trickle of casualties. Trench positions, covered by wire and minefields, were deeply dug and reminiscent of World War One. The line of the Forward Edge of the Battle Area ran roughly astride the 38th Parallel, and had been established after the succession of withdrawals and advances down and up the Korean peninsula after the initial offensive by the North Korea forces in June 1950. The normal problems of fighting at the end of a ten-thousand mile supply route had been exacerbated by the mountainous terrain, the intensely cold winters, the battle inoculation of new equipment (the Centurion tank), and the lack of proper winter clothing. Most of these problems had been resolved before our arrival. An understanding of the background to the operational climate is vital, and shows that our predecessors had much the worst of it.

It is timely that Captain Boardman has brought together many contributions, both external, and from surviving old comrades, before it is too late. Though already more than 30 books about the Korean War have been published, none has attempted to chronicle the Regiments' activities during the year through gathering individual memories, or to set our year in the context of the arduous campaign which, over eighteen months, had preceded it. We believe that this work will be of interest not only to survivors but to generations eager to understand what ancestors did, and to researchers wishing to gain the flavour of events through the recollections of those who were there.

Though Korea was the first attempt by the United Nations to resist aggression, it would be foolish to claim that there are political or operational lessons to be gleaned at this distance in time. The world today is very different, as is the British Army. The Regiment amalgamated in 1992 with The 4/7th Royal Dragoon Guards to form The Royal Dragoon Guards, who have already wide operational experiences in Iraq and Afghanistan in which the highest professional standards have been displayed, and their reputation assured. There may however be a few aspects of 1952 which will strike chords with current and future readers, whether military or civilian.

We all owe Captain Boardman our warmest thanks for the concept, and for pursuing its realisation with such enthusiasm, determination and zeal. His outstanding record as Regimental Secretary is complemented by his previous book "Tracks in Europe", and by this book.

The Korean survivors remember with lasting gratitude the good humour, spirit and professionalism of all ranks, often under difficult circumstances, and this includes those posted in from other Regiments and Corps for the year, who became in every way true "Skins" while with us.

This also pays a special tribute to the large body of National Servicemen who served loyally and faithfully in our ranks, and particularly those who volunteered to extend their service to three years on a "Gentleman's' Agreement" (which had no legal basis) so as to be eligible to remain with the Regiment for most of the tour. Their good humour and lively minds contributed to the high morale which animated all ranks. Many of the junior Non-Commissioned

Officers were National Service. The loyalty and professionalism of all the National Servicemen refuted the myths which then and since have portrayed them as reluctant conscripts carrying out meaningless tasks and training. This tribute is long overdue.

We record our deep thanks to those who have given so freely of their time and energy to read drafts and offer corrections, criticism or suggestions, in particular Major General GMG Swindells, Brigadier ATP Millen, Colonel CE Taylor, Colonel MJC Anstice and Mr D Pooley. Without their invaluable contributions and constructive comments the book would be inadequate and inaccurate.

We should also place on record what remarkable comradeship was evident throughout the Commonwealth Division which comprised Regiments, Battalions, detachments and individuals from almost every part of the Commonwealth. British and Australian Infantry, Canadian armour and infantry, Canadian and New Zealand gunners and the Indian Field Ambulance are some of those who served alongside us during 1952. Other Nations were envious of the strength of spirit which bonded our people together so effectively in their common allegiance to the Crown.

It would be insensitive not to pay tribute to the families and friends of all ranks who endured not only more than a year of separation, despite a speedy mail service (5days), but also very inferior married quarters and the disruption of family life and education, having left much higher standards in Germany. Their resilience, spirit and determination to make the best of what was available, reflects the greatest credit on them. Many spared their menfolk some of the problems they faced in order not to lower morale. All sought to help one another by mutual support.

We are profoundly grateful to those Korean Veterans who have shared their memories with us: the trouble they have taken deserves great praise and the anthology would not have been possible otherwise.

Since Captain Boardman began work, we sadly record the deaths of the following Korean veterans who had made important contributions to this work.

Brigadier A.T.Millen
Colonel MJC Anstice MC
Mr D Pooley

Lastly, though the scale of operations was less in 1952 than before, this anthology is a memorial to those who gave their lives during the year. On Remembrance Sundays families of those who perished and perhaps others will turn to the Roll of Honour, and reflect on the sacrifices made to bring about peace, then and more recently. This book is dedicated to All Ranks of the 5th Royal Inniskilling Dragoon Guards and attachments from other Regiments and Corps who served in Korea 1951-1952.

# "FARE THEE WELL, INNISKILLING"
## The Genesis of Tracks in Korea – An Anthology
### By
### Captain Jim Boardman

The challenge to bring together the memories of those who served in Korea during 1952 was thrown down at the Regimental Reunion after the Cavalry Memorial Service in Hyde Park in May 2010 by The Colonel of the Regiment, Brigadier Johnny Torrence Spence, HRH the Prince of Wales, our Colonel-in-Chief who had taken the Salute in the Park and attended the Reunion, had spoken to everyone as he moved round the room. Brigadier "Johnny" Torrens-Spence reminded us that 2012 would be the 60$^{th}$ anniversary of our year in Korea, and reported that consideration was being given to producing an account of that year. The Royal Dragoon Guards, then in Afghanistan, resulted from the amalgamation of the 4$^{th}$/7$^{th}$ Dragoon Guards and the 5$^{th}$ Royal Inniskilling Dragoon Guards in 1992. Sufficient enthusiasm and willingness to help was evident at the Reunion, and I answered the appeal for some-one to compile and edit the contributions. The task of seeking out those with a tale to tell and persuading them to put pen to paper has not been easy. It would have been much harder but for the help I have received from a wide range of former "Skins". Major General Henry Woods, who co-authored the most recent History of the 5$^{th}$ Royal Inniskilling Dragoon Guards – "Change and Challenge"- with General Sir Cecil Blacker, joined me in the vital stage of collating the memories and checking the drafts as well as the Foreword. We are particularly grateful to the following distinguished senior Officers, who were Troop Leaders in 1952, and assisted in the editorial phase;

Major General Michael Swindells, who has held high positions in

The Army Benevolent fund, the British Korean Veterans Association and the Royal British Legion.

Brigadier Anthony Millen, who contributed to the Anthology.

Colonel Charles Taylor, who was awarded the Military Cross.

Colonel Michael Anstice, who was also awarded the Military Cross, supporting The Black Watch during "The Hook" battle (subsequently added to our Battle Honours). Sadly, he and Anthony Millen died suddenly during the final stages of publication, and this will remain their epitaph.

In addition Sergeant Don Pooley has contributed and helped in all sorts of ways, but also died during the last phase prior to publication.

Photographs have been provided from Regimental Scrapbooks and the personal collections of Signalman Ian Stratford, Trooper John Cottrell and the late Sergeant Don Pooley. Propaganda pamphlets donated by the Spilsby Branch of The British Korean Veterans Association.

During my time as Regimental Secretary I was in contact with The Royal Australian Regiment and the Canadian Regiments whom we supported, and we are most grateful for their help. To all those who have contributed in one way or another, including those named at the head of each piece, we extent our warmest thanks; without them there would have been no anthology.

I visited The National Memorial Arboretum, the largest Memorial in Britain, commemorating all who gave their lives in every conflict including Korea since 1945. I realised that this wonderful oasis of peace and calm will be the focus of remembrance for future generations. During this anniversary year (2012) we are fortunate that another distinguished "Skin" and Commander 7th Armoured Brigade in the first Gulf War, Major General Patrick Cordingley, himself an author and broadcaster, is its Chairman. I was not alone! Perhaps any musical should include new words to "Thank Heaven for little girls" to be rendered as "Thank Heaven for junior officers who grow up in such an influential way"!

The National Arboretum, Staffordshire.

Korea past and present is akin to an up- draught creating a downdraught on the side of a mountain. Sources of the kind we were seeking ranged from published works such as the memoirs of the Revd. Sam Davies, the Chaplain of the 1st Battalion The Gloucester Regiment, our own Regimental History – "Change and Challenge", to the Regimental Journal for 1952, the Australian Service Journals and the Monthly Reports submitted to DRAC and other parts of the Chain of Command. The task was made more daunting as time has taken its toll, and many of the National Servicemen posted in from other Regiments left us to return to civilian life, doubtless excising from their memories the tribulations of 60years ago. Many have nevertheless continued to attend Association gatherings and are still in touch.

Colonel Guy Wathen succinctly described the Korean War as a Subaltern's campaign, and, as the Squadrons supported the Brigades of 1 Commonwealth Division, they led separate lives and apart from contact at reliefs, hardly saw one another throughout the year until they met on the train to Pusan on our departure. During one of my daily visits as Squadron Quarter Master Sergeant I remember joining a Troop Leader looking across the deep valley with terraced "Paddy Fields" to the opposite hills. He said "here we are with complete air supremacy, reasonable roads, well-fed and with the protection of four inches of armour; over there are North Koreans and Chinese who are lightly armed, and for sustenance have a pocketful of rice and we are stymied".

Korea was on the far side of the world, producing little in 1952 except rice and cereals. There were voices raised to doubt the wisdom of our involvement. Looking back now, we can see that the Korean War was pivotal in limiting the spread of communism, especially in the Far East. There was still a long road to travel through the Malayan insurgency and Vietnam, not to mention Cambodia, before we reached 1989 and the collapse of the Soviet Union. Today South Korea is a modern prosperous industrial giant, with the prestige gained by hosting the Olympic Games in 1988, and many sporting successes. Likewise China is now a military and economic superpower, with the success of the Beijing Olympics to increase her self-confidence. North Korea broods jealously north of the 38th Parallel with an Army of over a million men and its nuclear weapons but a starving population, and well aware that South Korea flourishes. We can proudly claim that our contribution played a part in that.

# ACKNOWLEGEMENT OF COPYRIGHTS

Despite a wide search to avoid any possible infringement of copyright regulations, no any one person or organisation has been discovered. The Intellectual Property Office advised that the written work of an author is entitled to protection lasts for the life of the author plus 70 years after the year of their passing. The following organisations and individuals have given their consent;

The Royal Australian Regiment:

Leading articles and statistics and including "Enter the Chinese" and "An Infantry Patrol". Published in their Regimental Journals, "Duty First" in 1992, 1993, 2008 and 2009.

The Kings Royal Irish Hussars:

The Home Headquarters of the Queens Royal Irish Hussars.

Extracts from their Regimental History, entitled "Men of Valour".

"In Spite of Dungeons" by the Rev "Sam" Davies. Deceased 2002. His son and daughter.

All other articles were supplied by the person whose name heads the story.

# ACKNOWLEDGEMENTS

I am deeply grateful to so many whose invaluable help has enabled us to bring together these memories sixty years on. Living 100 miles from our Home Headquarters in York meant that I have sought the support of my family, and thanks to the IT skills of my daughter, Janet, my almost illegible longhand has been transcribed and passed to the expert attention of Linda Watson in the HHQ. When Janet was away, my son David took on the support role; they were the two children I left behind in 1951. The final proofing was assisted by grandson James. When In York, Major Graham Green and Captain Alan Henshall have done so much to support the work at the publication stage.

All who have contributed and those who have checked the text and advised us on errors deserve our gratitude. Our particular thanks go to those who granted us permission to publish extracts from their published works.

Any remaining errors are the responsibility of the joint compilers, Major General Henry Woods and myself.

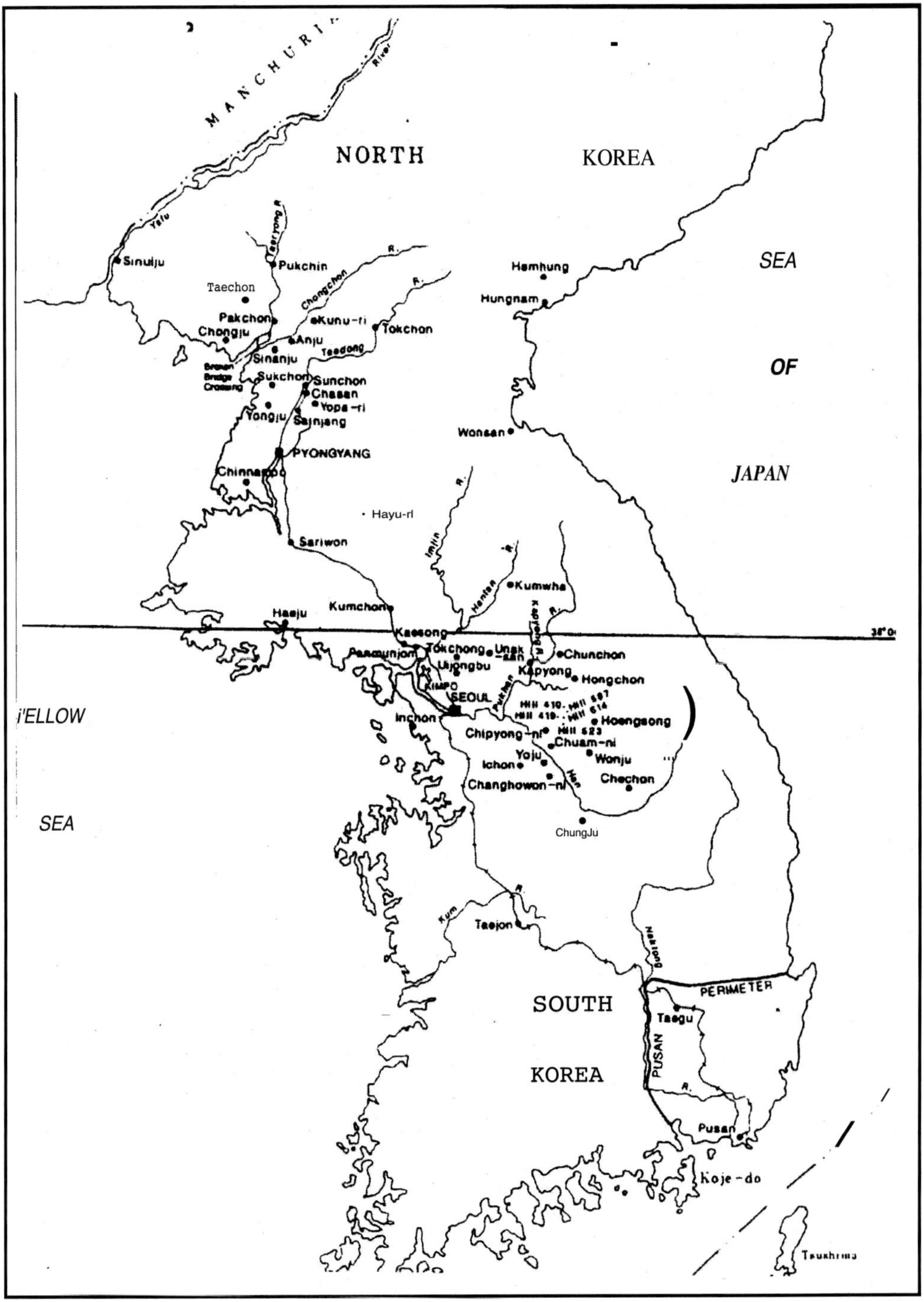

# UN FORCES CONTRIBUTIONS

Where no departure dates are shown, the regiments concerned departed after the ceasefire in July 1953. The exact dates are not known.

| | |
|---|---|
| **27 Comwel Brigade** | **August 50 – April 51** |
| **(27 Infantry Brigade until September 50)** | |
| 1 Middlesex | August 50 – Apr 51 |
| 1 Argyll & Sutherland Highlanders | August 50 – Apr 51 |
| 3 Royal Australian Regiment | September 50 – Apr 51 |
| 2 Princess Patricia Canadian Light Infantry | February 51 – Apr 51 |
| **28 Comwel Infantry Brigade** | **Apr 51** |
| 3 Royal Australian Regiment | April 51 |
| 2 Princess Patricia Canadian Light Infantry | April 51 – May 51 |
| 1 Kings Own Scottish Border | April 51 – Aug 52 |
| 1 Kings Shropshire Light Infantry | May 51 – September 52 |
| 1 Royal Australian Regiment | April 52 – Mar 53 |
| 1 Royal Fusiliers | August 52 – |
| 1 Durham Light Infantry | September 52 – |
| 2 Royal Australian Regiment | March 52 – |
| **29 Brit Infantry Brigade** | **November 50** |
| 1 Northumberland Fusiliers | November 50 – Oct 51 |
| 1 Gloucestershire Regt | November 50 – Oct 51 |
| 1 Royal Ulster Rifles | November 50 – Oct 51 |
| 1 Royal Norfolk | October 51 – September 52 |
| 1 Leicesters | October 51 – June 52 |
| 1 Welch Regt | November 51 – November 52 |
| 1 Black Watch | July 52 – |
| 1 The Kings Regt | September 52 – |
| 1 The Duke of Wellington | September 52 |

# UN FORCES CONTRIBUTION

**25 Canadian Infantry Brigade** — May 51 –
2 Princess Patricia Canadian Light Infantry — May 51 – November 52
2 Royal Canadian Regiment — May 51 – November 52
2 Royal 22e Regiment Vingt-deux — May 51 – April 52
1 Princess Patricia Canadian Light Infantry — October 51 – November 52
1 Royal Canadian Regiment — April 52 – November 53
1 Royal 22e Regiment Vingt-deux — April 52 – April 53
3 Princess Patricia Canadian Light Infantry — October 52 –
3 Royal Canadian Regiment — November 53 –
3 Royal 22e Regt Vingt-deux — April 53
**1 Comwel Div** — 28 July 51 –

**Armoured Units**
8 Kings Royal Irish Hussars — November 50 – December 51
'C' Squadron 7 Royal Tank Regiment — November 50 – Oct 51
5 Royal Inniskilling Dragoon Guards — December 51 – December 52
1 Royal Tank Regiment — December 52 –
'C' Squadron
Lord Strathcona's Horse — May 51 – June 52
B Squadron Lord Strathcona's Horse — June 52 – 53

**Artillery Units**
45 Field Regt Royal Artillery — November 50 – November 52
11 Independent Light Anti-Aircraft Battery — November 50 – October 51
170 Independent Mortar Battery Royal Artillery — November 50 – October 51
16th Field Regiment Royal New Zealand Army — January 51 –
2 Regiment Royal Canadian Horse Artillery — May 51 – May 52
14 Field Regiment Royal Artillery — November 51 – December 52
61 Light Regiment — January 52 –
20 Field Regiment Royal Artillery — December 52 –
1st Royal Canadian Horse Artillery — May 52 – April 55
81st Field Regiment Royal Canadian Artillery — April 53

**Engineers**
55 Field Squadron Royal Engineers — November 50 – July 51

TRACKS IN KOREA

57 Canadian Independent Field Squadron   November 50 – July 51
Above units amalgamated Jul 51 on formation of 1 Commonwealth Division to form 28th Field Brigade.

**Medical**

| | |
|---|---|
| 60th Para Ind Field Amb | November 50 – |
| 26th Field Amb RAMC | December 50 – |
| 25th Field Amb RCAMC | May 51 – April 52 |
| 24 Canadians FDS | July 51 |
| 37 Field Amb RCAMC | April 52 – May 53 |
| 38 Field Amb RCAMC | May 53 |

**Logistics**

| | |
|---|---|
| AAC | Army Air Corps |
| REME | Royal Electrical and Mechanical Engineers |
| RASC | Royal Army Services Club |
| RAOC | Royal Army Ordinance corps |
| RADC | Royal Army Dental Corps |
| ACC | Army Catering Corps |

******

**AUSTRALIA:** 2 Infantry Battalions, part of the 1st Commonwealth Division; 2 destroyers or frigates; 1 Aircraft Carrier and a Fighter Squadron.

**BELGIUM:** One reinforced Infantry Brigade, including tank and artillery forces, part of the 1st Commonwealth Division; 3 Destroyers; and a Squadron of Transport Aircraft.

**CANADA:** 1 reinforced Infantry Brigade, including Tank and Artillery Forces, part of the 1st Commonwealth Division; 3 Destroyers; and a Squadron of Transport Aircraft.

**COLOMBIA:** 1 Infantry Battalion and a Frigate.

**FRANCE:** 1 reinforced Infantry Battalion.

**GREECE:** 1 Infantry Battalion and Transport Aircraft.

**LUXEMBOURG:** 1 Infantry Platoon.

# UN FORCES CONTRIBUTION

**NETHERLANDS**: 1 Infantry Battalion and Naval Forces.

**NEW ZEALAND**: 1 Regiment of Artillery, part of the 1st Commonwealth Division.

**PHILIPPINES**: 1 Infantry Battalion and 1 Company of Tanks. **THAILAND**: 1 Infantry Battalion; Naval Forces, Air and Travel Transports.

**TURKEY**: 1 Infantry Brigade.

**UNION OF SOUTH AFRICA**: 1 Fighter Squadron.

**UNITED KINGDOM**: 2 Infantry Brigades, 1 Armoured Regiment, 1½ Engineer Regiments and supporting ground forces, all part of the 1st Commonwealth Division; British Far East Fleet; and Sunderland Aircraft of the RAF. 1 Flight Army Air Corps.

**UNITED STATES OF AMERICA**: The 8th Army, of 6 Army Divisions and 1 Marine Division; Naval Forces Far East (3 Task Forces); and Far East Air Forces (3 Air Forces).

**DENMARK, ITALY, INDIA, NORWAY and SWEDEN** contributed Medical Units.

## CASUALTIES

It is estimated that over 2 million and probably as many as 4 million lost their lives during this three year campaign of which 1,092 were British.

USA lost c. 36,500.

North Korea and China c.600,000

South Korea c.138,000

# PROGRESSION TO CONFLICT

In 1950 the world was still in a state of chaos. Countries occupied by Germany or Japan, which had been mandated to other countries after The Great War, wanted independence. There were internal struggles for power under different parties; France in North Africa, Belgium in the Congo, Holland in the East Indies. India had gained independence from Great Britain and a new state, Pakistan, had been established. Malaya was fighting a communist uprising. Hong Kong and Singapore, now also wanted independence. All countries had difficulties to address. America had a witch hunt to identify Communist sympathisers and China fought a Communist versus Nationalist war. All countries were affected, even those who had been neutral, Sweden, Switzerland, Portugal, Spain and Ireland. Priority had been given to rebuilding our industry and to our destroyed cities and to creating employment for our vast wartime army. The main aggressor was Joseph Stalin, the brutal dictator of the Soviet Union, who had annexed satellite states in Eastern Europe. There were atrocities in Czechoslovakia, Poland and Hungary. We had maintained a large army and had the training facilities but those countries which had been occupied had to depend upon America and Britain for most of their equipment. We also had a large shipping fleet despite some of it being mothballed in places like Harwich Harbour. It is of great credit that so many small countries gave such valuable support to the United Nations, Greece and Belgium for example. Belgian troops suffered badly at the hands of the Chinese and at that time we had a close affiliation; King Leopold III of the Belgians was the Colonel in Chief of the 5th Royal Inniskilling Dragoon Guards, as had been King Leopold 1st. We were personally involved. Of course we had a reason to counter this aggression! The Korean War was now to be firmly part of our Regimental History and later, The Royal Dragoon Guards'. It is necessary to back track to events which led to our intervention.

# THE NORTH KOREAN INVASION

The following articles were part of the coverage given in the Australian Forces Magazine, 'Duty First'. With the maps they give a clear account of the Chinese attack and subsequent battles prior to the arrival of the 5th Royal Inniskilling Dragoon Guards in December 1951.

Korea was occupied by the Japanese during the Second World War. The Communist North was on the southern boundaries of the Soviet Empire and supported by the USSR. This led to an attempt to occupy South Korea which was occupied by American Troops. The two countries were poles apart and have continued to be so.

\* \* \* \* \* \*

General Douglas MacArthur had asked for and was initially given permission to defend the South with nuclear weapons. This authorisation was later withdrawn and General MacArthur replaced by General Ridgeway. On 25 June 1950, the North invaded the South. The Russians supported the North. The United Nations re-enforced the South.

\* \* \* \* \* \*

The 27th Brigade from Hong Kong was never intended to be part of the original United Kingdom commitment to the UN Forces, the original commitment was to have been a Brigade Group, the 29th, consisting

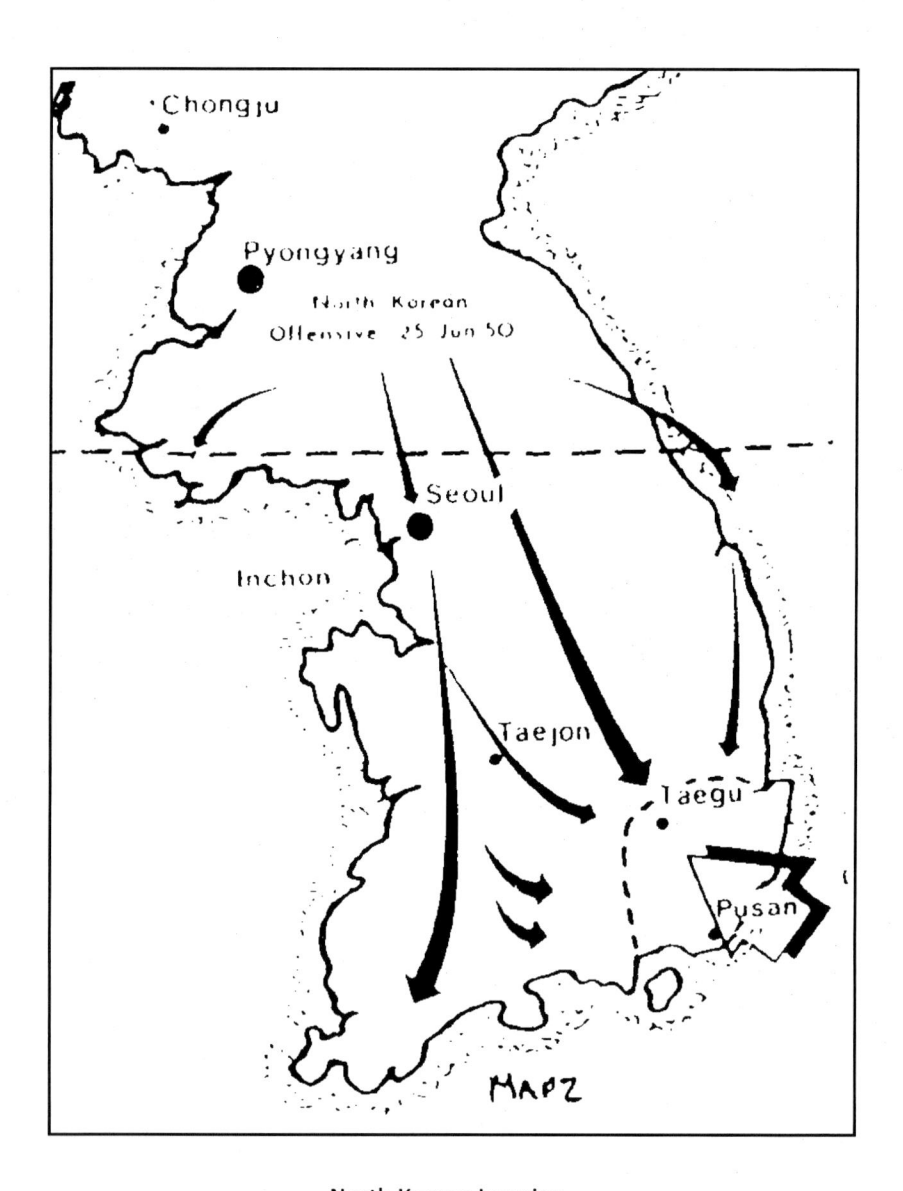

North Korean Invasion.

of: 3 Infantry Battalions, a Field Artillery Regiment, a 4.2 Mortar/LAA Battery, 'A' Squadron of 7th Royal Tank Regiment, and a Squadron of Engineers. Later this was amended to include a Divisional HQ, an HQ RA, plus supporting services. The 29th Brigade was activated in the UK in response to the UN Secretary's request, made on 29th June 1950, calling on all member nations for assistance. On the same day Prime Minister RG Menzies announced that two Australian warships, presently in Japanese waters, had been placed at the disposal of UN Forces. Later that day Lieutenant General Sir Horace Robertson, Commanding the British Commonwealth Occupation Forces in Japan, ordered 77 Fighter Squadron RAAF to a state of war readiness. The following day he placed 77 Sqn RAAF under UN Command.

By the 17 July 1950, with the American Troops holding the perimeter around Pusan, General Douglas MacArthur made an appeal for immediate assistance. In Hong Kong, at 10pm on Saturday 19th July the CO's of the Argyll's, and the Middlesex were summoned to report to Brigade HQ at 9am the following day. During the sombre meeting with Brigade Major Jimmy Stewart, the Battalion Commanding Officers were told that the depleted Brigade would embark on the Aircraft Carrier HMS Unicorn and Cruiser HMS Ceylon the following Friday 25th August. The Commanding Officers were told that they were to be a token force, for a limited period, in an emergency situation pending the arrival of the 29th Brigade from the UK.

The UN counterattacked northwards in the early spring of 1951 and by December the UN Forces held a well-established defended area roughly along the 38th Parallel just north of the River Imjin and about 50 miles beyond the South Korean capital of Seoul, despite local Chinese offensives such as their Corps attack on the 29th Infantry Brigade along the River Imjin in the previous April, in which the Gloucesters had won fame. The British and Commonwealth contributions to the UN military effort had consolidated into 1st Commonwealth Division, consisting of three Brigades, 25th (Canadian), 28th (British, Australian and New Zealand) and 29th (British).

Prior to his dismissal, by President Truman for insubordination, General MacArthur had retrieved the situation by a daring landing close to Seoul, 300 kilometres behind the communist lines. The UN troops had regained the initiative and pushed the North Koreans as far as the Yalu River on the Sino-Korean border. This break-through unleashed great optimism. Diplomacy was neglected and the military operation became even bolder. The Chinese intervention took the UN force by surprise. They hastily withdrew and abandoned Seoul once again. The communist troops were halted on a defensive line south of the occupied capital. This was the situation when reinforcements landed on 31 January 1951.

# KOREA – ENTER THE CHINESE
## By Russell Spurr

The following are condensed segments from Russell Spurr's book 'Enter the Dragon' based upon interviews with Chinese veterans who presented their view of China's entry into the Korean War. The book traces the impact of the initial Chinese offensives, through the recapture of Seoul, to the UN counterattack that turned the tide of battle in February 1951.

General Peng Dehuai watched his men streaming out across the Yalu bridges. Like Caesar's Rubicon, the Yalu River marked an historic boundary whose crossing created irrevocable commitments. The General shook his head regretfully. He needed time, more time. Chinese entry into Korea had been brought forward a week because the Americans and their allies were advancing faster than expected across the 38th Parallel, the dividing line between South and North Korea, following the collapse of the North Korean offensive after the Inchon landing. The date was 14th October 1950. The Chinese were ill prepared, but now there could be no turning back. China was committed to rescuing their Korean comrades from total destruction by what they called 'Western Imperialism'.

Troops now filing across the bridges belonged to the 334th Regiment, 112th Division of the 38th Field Army. Two other Field Armies, the 39th and the 40th, would follow them into beleaguered Korea, while at Manpojin, 160kms further east, the 42 Field Army, would cross simultaneously. Together they would advance down either coast of the Korea peninsula to block the enemy advance. Two more Field Armies, the 50th and 66th, would follow before the months end, bringing Chinese military strength in North Korea to 380,000 men.

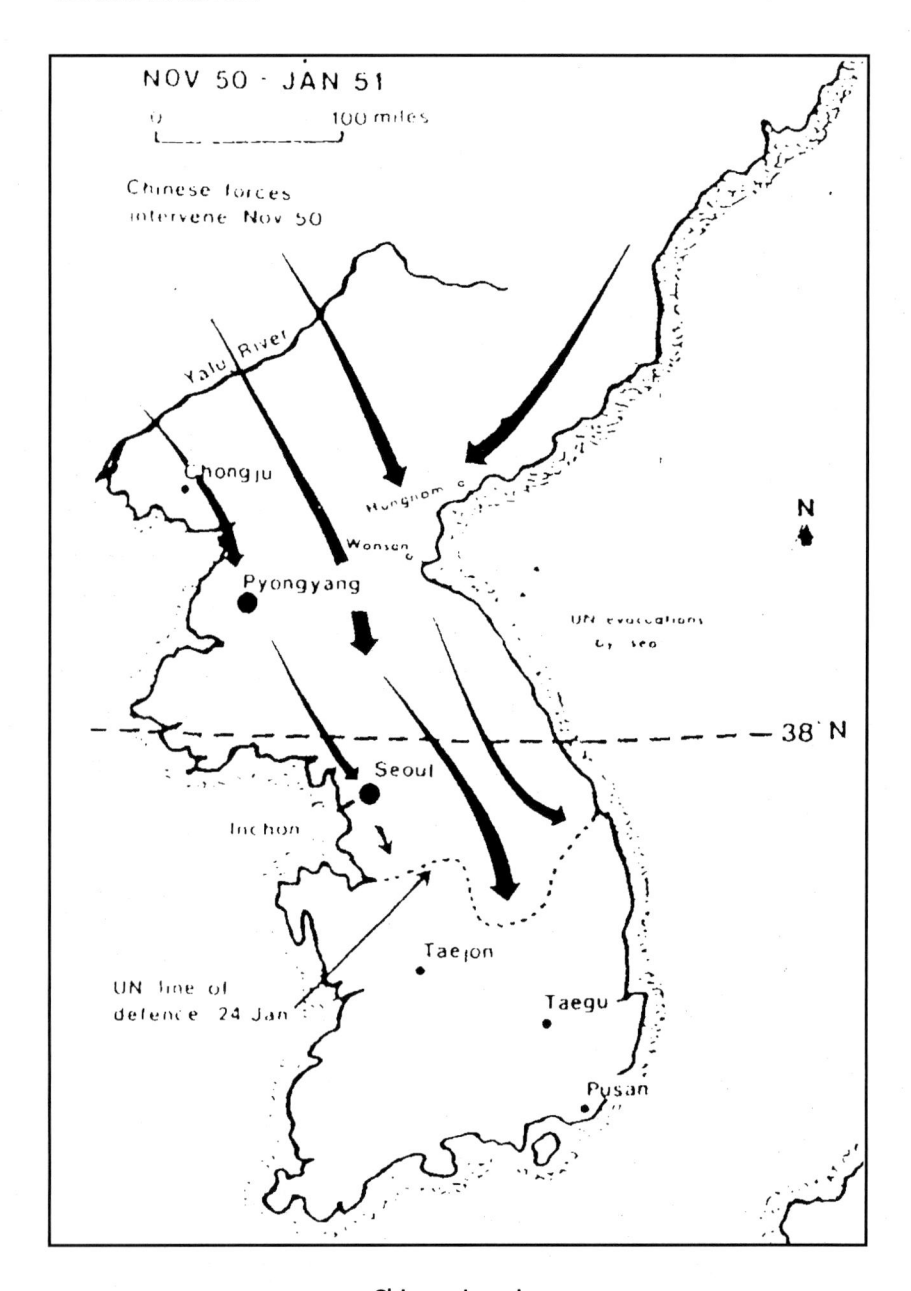

Chinese Invasion.

# KOREA – ENTER THE CHINESE

General Peng had emphasised the size and complexity of the operation at his final command briefing. He had stressed the desirability of mobility and surprise. The inadequacy of his forces, the so-called Chinese Peoples' Volunteers, was tactfully ignored although the General was undoubtedly aware of them. The risks of committing an Army of Infantrymen, no matter how numerous, against the firepower of the greatest military power on earth were offset by hopes that the Americans would be caught completely off-guard.

Colonel Yang Shixian was halfway across the Yalu when the sirens sounded on the Chinese side of the river. A bugler high up on the bridge blew a short warning blast. Everybody froze, faces down, the way they had rehearsed it in Manchuria. Colonel Yang waited with bated breath for the growl of aeroplane engines, the whistle of falling bombs. Instead, the sound of motors died away. The unseen bugler sounded the all clear.

It would take Colonel Yang's men 5 hours to get across. The 2nd Battalion, the 347th Regt, 116th Division, was stretched out for at least a couple of kilometres. The rear-guard was shuffling along somewhere back in the Chinese rail yards. Two files negotiated the catwalks on each side of the bridge, some laden with metal cook pots that clanged against the metalwork. The Colonel was anxious to get his men across without further alarm. He chuckled politely to the reception committee, handed his bouquet to his Orderly and strode smartly onto North Korean soil.

That first step would be his minor contribution to history. He had been wondering for weeks what it would be like. Surprisingly, the river bank felt no different from the Chinese side – soggy and half frozen – although the town of Sinuiju was badly battered. The American bombers had done a formidable job. Most of the buildings were bombed or burned or both. There was no triumphal march down the high street. Military Police diverted the Chinese through the western industrial suburbs. They were 6kms beyond Sinuiju before the Colonel called a halt.

But not for long ... the North Korean guide, who spoke excellent Chinese, was anxious to get them concealed deep in the countryside. There were still 16kms to go. The going grew tougher as they groped their way along narrow, stony paths. Night fell, there was no moon, but the clouds were gone. The sky was bright with stars. North Koreans kept appearing from the Shadows to guide them with remarkable efficiency. They ran white tapes across the hills. Men and women with masked lanterns pointed the way through the most difficult terrain.

It was getting on towards 2200 hours when the Battalion reached a shallow, pine-clad valley within the foothills. Everyone was dead weary, especially Colonel Yang. It had been a long unnerving day. The cooks greeted them under the trees with a dinner prepared. A scattering of tents ran up the hillside swathed in camouflage netting. Coded signals came over the radio ordering a resumption of the march the following night. There was no time to lose, the signals emphasised, because the Americans had taken Pyongyang and were advancing rapidly north. The enemy Commander, MacArthur, was determined to drive to the Yalu River. The whole of North Korea would then be in his hands.

"At this rate", Colonel Yang told his staff, "we'll be in action in a week". The staff nodded eager assent. Now the dice were rolled they could not wait to get to grips with the Yankees.

The Chinese Peoples Volunteers were ordered to make limited strikes against the advancing UN Forces. The 166th Division was targeted against the 8th Regiment, US 1st Cavalry Division at Unsan. The South Koreans on 1st Cavalry's flank was also earmarked for destruction. The recently formed Republic of Korea (ROK) Forces were considered an easy option by the communists. The plan was to infiltrate a commando unit into the American defensive position around midnight, 1 November 1950, while Colonel Yang's troops moved round to ambush the Americans' along the single escape route.

The offensive had so far gone incredibly well, so well that Colonel Yang might well have felt elated. But the last dash up the hill had left him winded. He had managed to keep pace with his men over the first kilometre or so, creeping through the rice fields past unsuspecting Unsan. The climb up this miserable hill reminded him, however, that he was no longer the youthful hero of a 100 battles. He was 43 and feeling faintly sick.

The Colonel's own quarry, the trapped Americans of the First Cavalry Division, were scattering in some disorder around Unsan. They were a tough outfit. The 39th Field Army Commander, Major General Wu Xinzhan, had made that clear at the briefing. The 39th Field Army had been chosen, as the most experienced in China, to launch the first blow against the enemy.

An explosion from the direction of Unsan sent up a shower of sparks. The Commando Squad was tossing satchel charges into the American store dumps. The growl of revving engines rumbles up from behind the hill. The Americans were pulling out. A jeep swung into sight along the empty road. Its windshield was locked down on the hood. The jeep bulged with armed men. Yang held his breath. The trick was to wait for the main convoy. No-one was to open fire until he gave the order. The bugler crouched expectantly at his elbow.

The jeep stopped. It backed up a few metres. An American climbed out and waved at something or someone farther down the road. "He's calling the convoy", whispered Yang. The American suddenly jumped back into the jeep. He pointed wildly toward the river. Shots rang out from a line of Chinese riflemen approaching in full view across the rice fields. The jeep shot away round the bend. The roar of many over-gunned engines echoed through the valley as the convoy came racing in pursuit. The big enemy trucks attempted to drive on through, led by a 2½ Tonner towing a 105 mm howitzer whose dull steel tube gleamed in the moonlight.

Colonel Yang gestured to the bugler, who sprang defiantly against the skyline. With one hand on hip, one hand holding the red-tasselled bugle to his lips, the bugler blew short blasts that unleashed a hurricane of small arms fire upon the speeding vehicles. Windshields shattered, radiators exploded, and men dived onto the road to escape the fusillade. The lead truck swerved off the embankment and nose-dived into the rice field. The howitzer jack-knifed, blocking the road. Further back, one truck rammed the rear of another. A jeep trying to edge past and sort out the mess slid off the road and overturned.

The Americans sought cover behind their stalled vehicles. But by now they were under fire from both sides of the road. The trapped men fought back gamely. Tracer came whipping up the hill finding an occasional Chinese target. A messenger running up from the mortar squad staggered and pitched forward. Whatever word he was carrying would never be relayed.

Two days later the battle ended. Orders came through to break off and withdraw. The Americans had been duly warned against attempting further advance. But General MacArthur refused to believe the Chinese had entered Korea in any strength. His Chief of Staff flew over from Tokyo and upbraided the UN Command. "Afraid of a few Chinese Laundrymen?" he sneered. After celebrating Halloween the UN advance resumed. According to MacArthur it would "end the war by Christmas". This time the Chinese attacked in overwhelming strength.

Colonel Yang Shixian stared impatiently down into the still dark valley. The date was 27 November. His watch said 0507. The Colonel was waiting for the explosions. When they came he would know the infiltration squads had done their work. He tried peering again through his binoculars. Tents, trucks and guns were all he could see, blurred by the soft ground mist. Suddenly, a stir of movement, men running, a series of flashes in the darkness, followed a few moments later by the dull crump of the satchel charges. A burst of flame as a truck caught fire. An outburst of ragged shooting, he nodded curtly to the bugler.

The call to the charge brayed urgently off the mountain top. Other distant buglers took up the sound, spreading their staccato message across the mountain slopes. The sounds had scarcely died away when the mountains moved. Ridges cloaked in rock and scrub swarmed suddenly with Chinese soldiers in bulky padded jackets. An avalanche of soldiers with rifles and fixed bayonets emerged yelling from concealment and goat-leaped down the slope. With battle irrevocably joined, he felt the old familiar feelings of relief. Vast trouble had been taken to arrive here undetected from the ravine where they had rested for 3 weeks following the Unsan battle. It was good to be active again after so much cowering under camouflage. Someone was sounding a gong. Others blew whistles. But there was no artillery preparation; the nearest Chinese guns were stuck somewhere near the Yalu. The Chinese surprise attack, mounted purely by unsupported infantry, was reminiscent of the American Civil War; European Armies had not fought this way this century.

The enemy was firing wildly and without effect. The explosions inside their perimeter must have unnerved them. The Colonel was less than 100 metres from the foremost foxholes when something exploded inside the South Korean Camp. The defenders stopped shooting and fled. They leaped from their foxholes and blundered off through the tents and trucks towards the rear. They ran in blind panic, heads down and crouching, leaving a trail of helmets, packs, and rifles. Unknown to them the road to the rear was already cut.

The 2nd Battalion, 347th Regiment, regrouped excitedly in the growing light. The Chinese soldiers were plainly delighted with their initial success. A South Korean Regiment HQ had been overrun in those first few hectic minutes. Right now, however, the Chinese were starving. They'd eaten nothing during their covert advance of the past 2 days. The rush began to loot the captured dumps of enemy supplies. The bulk of the rations appeared to be American. The only recognisable foodstuffs, mostly rice and several pots of Kimchee, were obviously Korean. GIs ate the oddest things, the Chinese remarked. There was much more meat than they were used to, but remarkably few vegetables. Some of the rations proved more popular than others. Everyone clamoured for candles and cans containing sliced peaches, and something with an unknown Mexican name appealed to men such as the Colonel who enjoyed spicier food. Most of the other stuff was considered tasteless.

Captured ammunition stocks were the next to be plundered. Search parties gathered up bundles of abandoned carbines and M-1 rifles. The Chinese disliked the carbine. They felt it packed too little stopping power. But the M-1 rifle was greatly prized. The few infantrymen still using Japanese and Chinese made rifles traded them in for M-1s, with orders to keep foraging for further ammunition supplies. The ammunition shortage was serious. Each man carried four clips of M-1 rounds, with instructions never to fire except close to the enemy. Running down the hillside in the predawn attack the battalion had made plenty of noise but expended relatively few rounds.

The Chinese attacked without the essentials of modern war. They attacked without aircraft, artillery or tanks. They lacked sophisticated communications and logistics. But they had ample manpower. They threw 6 field armies – totalling some 180,000 men – down the western side of the Korea peninsula in an effort to engulf the US 8th Army. Three of those field armies blocked the path of 3 American Divs advancing to the Chinese border from the Chungchon River. Farther inland, where awesome mountains divide the peninsula, 3 more Chinese field armies hammered the ill-fated South Koreans. The ROK II Corps crumbled and the Chinese poured through the gap and launched an outflanking movement that threatened the UN escape route to the south. By the evening of 26 November, it became apparent to those in the field that MacArthur's end-the-war drive to the Yalu had failed.

\* \* \* \* \* \*

On 20 April 1951, the Gloucestershire Regiment, 29th British Brigade had dug in for what was to be the hardest and most heroic battles of the Korean War. At that point, a major Chinese offensive to push the UN troops decisively back into the sea was being mounted. On 22 April, 50,000 Chinese attacked the 29th Brigade which was getting ready to celebrate St George's Day (the Gloucester's patron). That plan was hastily dropped in the face of more immediate needs. At 6am, the battalion was surrounded.

This assault gave the Chinese a chance to take a few prisoners who were shot. Their bodies were found after a subsequent counterattack.

The rest of the Brigade was also in a very critical situation. The surrounded Gloucester Regiment could not be relieved despite vigorous efforts by the Belgians, the Filipinos and the 8th King's Royal Hussars. It was left to its fate and almost annihilated after an extraordinary display of courage and dignity.

The Brigade was finally relieved on 26th April, 6 days after taking up position.

# Korean War: The Battle of The Imjin

# THE IMJIN BATTLE

The Reverend 'Sam' Davies, Padre to the Gloucester's related with the moving story of the initial attack, the heroic defence and his suffering as a Prisoner of War. His book, 'In Spite of Dungeons' is compulsive reading. A story of suffering and the ability to survive. I have chosen to reprint the first chapter exactly as he wrote it:

"Twilight was falling on the Imjin River, bringing the grey, chilly April evening to a close. The last of the returning 'Centurions' lurched across the shallows like gigantic beetles, their antennæ waving. All day, from crack of dawn, they had probed deep into the 'No Man's Land' across the Imjin, carrying with them a strong task force of Gloucester's. There had been desultory firing, and the infantry had swarmed without opposition across several trenched slopes. No contact was made with the Chinese. Everywhere naïvely-worded leaflets were found urging the United Nations' troops to give up the fight, and telling them this was a war for the blood-soaked profits of Morgan, Dupont and Rockefeller. Safe conduct was guaranteed to those who surrendered in possession of the leaflet.

It was good to be back on 'our side' of the Imjin; good to sip steaming cocoa in the candlelight, and fall asleep with the comforting knowledge that the Chinese Communist forces were miles away beyond the broad river. The date was Friday 20th April 1951.

The 5th Fusiliers lay along the Imjin almost 5 miles to the Gloucesters' right flank. Lieutenant Colonel Kingsley Foster had invited me to conduct and preach at their annual Saint George's Day Service, which was brought forward to Sunday 22nd April. The service was held in the open, at the foot of a steep hill. It was a clear, bracing morning. The strong, manly singing rose courageously into the blue. At the end, the Colonel proudly read the awards for service in Korea recently conferred on members of the Battalion by His Majesty. Afterwards we strolled to his tent for sherry. Two days later, the Colonel lay dead in his jeep, riddled with bullets, while the Chinese advance rolled on.

At midday I returned to my own Battalion, the Gloucesters. I set up my altar in a half ruined temple in 'A' Company's lines, overlooking the Imjin, and celebrated Holy Communion. Among the communicants able to attend were two young subalterns, Terry Waters and Philip Curtis. It was their Viaticum. That very night 'A', the Gloucesters' most forward company, was completely enveloped by the Chinese and subjected to a murderous assault. The Commander was killed. Philip Curtis proved an inspiration to his men. Early in the morning he, too, was killed, making a desperate, lone assault, already wounded, against a Chinese machine gun bunker. The Victoria Cross was conferred upon him posthumously in November 1953. Among his last acts on earth was the reception of the Blessed Sacrament at my hands.

Terry was the only Officer to survive. He got back with the remnants of the Company to Battalion HQ on the Monday morning. He died later in the year as a prisoner-of-war in the notorious 'Caves', near Pyongyang, having gallantly resisted all attempts by his North Korean captors to make him take part in propaganda work. In April 1954, he was posthumously awarded the George Cross. Terry was faced with the choice: "death or dishonour". He chose death.

Chatting and drinking tea together after the service, such endings to their young lives were unimaginable. As we stood in the sunny temple courtyard, word came that a Gloucester patrol across the Imjin was in contact with Chinese troops. The news caused no alarm; we received it carelessly. I bade them goodbye and returned by jeep to HQ.

That Sunday evening after nightfall, Guy, the Lieutenant in Command of the watching patrol at the river crossing, came back with his men. He was tense and excited. "At first", he said, "It looked like 10 or 20 coming across. We killed quite a few. Then I reckon hundreds of them were pouring across in the moonlight".

# THE IMJIN BATTLE

All around the vast black humps of the mountains seemed full of menace and foreboding. As I thought of 'A' Company lying in front of us in their positions overlooking the river, my stomach turned. The first staccato bursts of firing could be heard. The night came alive with the wicked chatter of small-arms a mile down the road. In bright moonlight the Chinese pushed up the long spur beyond 'A' Company, and began to attack 'D'. All companies became embroiled. Heavy fighting continued throughout the night in the high ground surrounding Battalion HQ. Friday's tank probe across the Imjin had revealed little: the enemy had evidently melted away only to surge swiftly forward under cover of darkness. As dawn broke, Mr Hobbs, the RSM, said to me over a cup of char: "They'll give up at dawn. Mark my words, sir; they'll go back across the river".

A few minutes later we went to ground as snipers' bullets whined overhead. Then silence.

The blessed light of day came: Saint George's Day, Monday 23rd April. Carriers, with Lieutenant Gabral in Command, set off down the road to extricate the survivors and wounded of 'A' Company. Firing had well-nigh ceased and the Chinese, fearing American air activity, had gone to ground. The men of 'Able' came in. They had taken terrible punishment, hour after hour, as the Chinese wave broke over them. Major Pat Angior's body was brought back. His batman was in tears. The bodies of Lieutenants Curtis and Maycock could not be retrieved. The ambulances began to evacuate the wounded. Now 'D' Company withdrew on HQ, their young subalterns cocky, the men cheerful and resolute after a gruelling night's fighting at close range. Although Colonel Carne looked tired, his face grave, there was an unruffled calmness about him that gave great reassurance. Fresh dispositions were allotted to 'A' and 'D' Companies. A little after midday the last ambulance pulled out. We prepared for the battle we knew would inevitably develop that night. There was a spirit of confidence in our ability to hold on.

At about 3 o'clock that Monday afternoon the last hurried message from Battalion Rear HQ came over the air. It informed us that Chinese troops, some 5 miles behind us, were attacking in greatly superior strength, and that the situation was desperate. The Battalion was cut off by a powerful and fast-moving enemy.

The road to safety was a tortuous one winding between steeply-rising mountain slopes: a paradise for guerrillas and enemy troops in ambush. Standing in the sunny hollow where main HQ lay I tried to realise the position. We were isolated by Chinese hordes intent on the kill. It was simply a matter of hours before darkness fell, and the lonely Battalion would be assaulted on all sides in the nightmarish moonlight. Gloucester was 11,000 miles away. I longed to be able to say 'Stop' to the rushing minutes: to prolong this quiet, sunny afternoon indefinitely.

A sinister hush seemed to lie in the towering mountains. Fear twisted inside me. The Battalion Doctor had carefully sewn up Major Angior's body in blankets. With the Adjutant, Tony Farrar-Hockley for congregation, I said the burial prayers. We bade farewell to Pat, laying his body out of the sun under an upturned assault-craft.

It grew to 5 o'clock and the troops queued for supper. In spite of the tense atmosphere everyone did his best to appear cheerful, but I found it impossible to enjoy the meal. The Adjutant moved about among the men, cracking jokes and dispersing many fears by his confident, bracing air and infectious smile. Night fell and the moon came up in its brilliance. Still all was quiet: the lull before the storm. At last the firing began in the surrounding heights: battle was joined. The mortars at HQ began to bark, lobbing their missiles over the shielding hill into the advancing Chinese.

After midnight, 'B' and 'C' Companies were under overwhelming pressure, and Battalion HQ was menaced. The Colonel was compelled to order evacuation of the perimeter. There was not a moment to lose. Still the mortar-gunners kept up their fire at the hoarse, strident Command of their Sergeant Major. The first Chinese bullets sang across the bowl in which HQ lay. The order was given to withdraw, and concentrate upon the high ground on our left flank. 'Support'

Company, and 'Able' and 'Dog' companies were already dug-in along the highest ridge. The Doctor loaded me with dressings, bandages and medical supplies, and we set off for the gully leading up to the ridge. My field Communion case had to be abandoned. The slope was alive with scrambling, panting men. It was a stiff climb, and the tracer bullets began to whip across, their red witch-balls floating eerily. At last we reached comparatively safe ground, a sheltered plateau high above the valley. Dawn broke.

'B' Company, isolated and battered by innumerable Chinese waves, now began to withdraw from their hill with as much cover from our machine-guns and artillery as possible. It was a run for it: a drama acted out far below us. At last Major Harding and 20 men reached the gully leading to our ground, and wearily rejoined the Battalion.

Throughout Tuesday we lay exposed on this high ground. Our snipers, under Henry Cabral's direction, were active with harassing fire whenever the Chinese showed themselves in the valley below. It was a fairly quiet day, blue and warm. The wounded were attended to and I conducted one burial. It was very difficult to dig even a shallow grave in the hard, rocky earth. During the morning, a smouldering fire among the brushwood began to spread ominously, fanned by the breeze. Here was yet another difficulty. A party was detailed to beat it out.

We lacked food, water, batteries and ammunition. Courageous men went down the gully with the Regimental Sergeant Major, and under cover from machine-gun and smoke, raided our old dug-outs and trucks still standing at the foot of the ridge. They barely had time to get the goods and a small supply of biscuits and bully-beef. There was now enough replenishment to ensure the encircled Battalion small-arms defence for a limited time.

Everyone was outwardly calm and still hopeful. The spirit of the affair is epitomised by the Adjutants' instructions to a subaltern of 'C' Company:

"Guy, you will stay here with your chaps unless you get orders from me to the contrary. If your ammunition runs out, hurl bloody rocks at them".

The signallers crouched over their gradually fading radios. Colonel Carne set his earphones on, in a small hollow, stolidly smoking the famous pipe. We knew that a strong relief column was attempting to get to us through the narrow defile. At first it was thought we might be relieved by midday. Noon came, and the men grew resigned. There was a report of a tank brewing-up, and blocking the advance of the rest. Everything seemed against us. It proved impossible for helicopters to land for our seriously wounded. The sense of our isolation became acute.

In the midst of all this, the spirit of the men of Gloucester Hill remained steady. A member of Support Company, being told by the Colonel that the whole Battalion would very soon be brought up to the higher ridge for the last fight, said cheerfully, "We shall be all right, sir, 'twill be like the Rock of Gibraltar up here".

I sat and read some old letters, afterwards tearing them up with an awesome sense of finality. Towards sunset, 'planes flew low over the ridge and attempted an airdrop. It was disheartening to see the bundles missing our positions and falling inaccessibly on the lower slopes. Fortunately, plasma and blood transfusion equipment landed safely. Immediately the Battalion Doctor was able to set to work, and save a dying man's life there on the ridge.

As twilight came, we withdrew from our positions and climbed in single file to the topmost ridge of 'Gloucester Hill' for the last desperate stand. It was a red sunset. The ridge commanded a superb view of the surrounding country and adjacent heights. In the darkness a thousand conflagrations, caused by napalm and shelling, glowed like campfires on the mountain slopes. We started to dig-in as best we could with the very few tools available. Everyone worked urgently with a driving sense of fear and necessity. I was only able to scrape a shallow trench in the stubborn ground. I walked about talking to men, trying to appear relaxed and hopeful, and feeling for encouraging words. It was far from easy. The medical aid post was sited in a hollow just below the line of the ridge. For most of the night this was my location.

A bugle shrilled in the darkness. Its haunting notes re-echoed and died away. Suddenly a light machine-gun started up its crackling chatter. Other weapons opened fire. The resonant stammering of the heavy machine-guns gave depth to the chorus. Shells from the British artillery, miles behind us, screamed weirdly over the ridge and crashed amidst the enemy on the slopes.

Along the ridge lay Battalion HQ, 'Support' Company, and in a small hollow the medical aid post. To the north lay 'Able' and 'Dog', to the south combined 'Baker-Charlie' Company and the mortar-gunners. The Chinese attacked from the south-east and up the approach from the north. The whole ridge of 'Gloucester Hill' was swept by enemy fire. Machine-guns were firing on fixed lines from a hill to our west, and the medical post and 'Support' Company's forward positions were threatened. At times, as the doctor and I lay in our shallow scrape, we could hear the bullets cutting the foliage some 4 feet above our heads. Mentally I prayed with a kind of fierce desperation. A more comforting sound was the rush and scream of our own shells, dropping to burst amidst the swarming enemy. We were within a curtain of steel.

From time to time, I heard the Adjutants' voice in different places in the darkness, shouting words of exhortation or advice to the hard-pressed troops. During the early hours, 'A' Company, which had already suffered so heavily, was exposed to a Chinese storming assault and fell back dangerously. Suddenly there rang out brazenly the long reveille blown by Drum-Major Buss. There was a cheer from the hill's defenders. With amazing impudence 'Drummie' followed this with 'Come to the cookhouse door boys', and then the whole run of Army calls.

At dawn, 'Able' counterattacked, under the Adjutants' leadership, with magnificent courage and retook much lost ground. Repeatedly assaulted, they were not dislodged and continued to cover the northerly approach to the vital ridge. 'D' Company was also taking heavy attack with a grim bravery. The southernmost defenders of the ridge were frequently disposed on forward slopes and from dawn were raked by heavy machine-gun and mortar fire. This they returned with great effect, but ammunition was running low and casualties mounted steadily. Our Signals Officer, Richard Reeve-Tucker, was killed instantaneously at this time. With almost irritating nonchalance, the Colonel moved to and fro in view of his men, amidst the hail.

In the cold morning light we awaited relief by a regimental combat team of the 3rd US Infantry Division. There was no food, and virtually no water. Wireless batteries were almost done. An impenetrable mist heaved below us like a sea of mil, blotting out all sight of the valley. As I crouched amidst a group of wounded I went back in memory to a skiing holiday at Chamonix. I remembered swinging up to the mountain top at Les Houches in the cable-cabin, and looking out over just such a rolling, milky vista, just as we saw now. An American 'plane swooped above us, so close we could see the pilot at the controls. He turned and ran in again. I waved my white handkerchief. Oh desperation, so close and yet so far! Mr Hobbs called out, "They're coming up on all sides! A rich Gloucestershire voice shouted: "Come on then, you bastards, and get your breakfast". Chinese bugles sounded their slow, haunting notes hanging in the sharp air. American 'planes roared from the sky, strafing and rocketing with incredible precision all along the sides of the ridge. It was an inferno of tearing, screaming sound. Napalm scorched and seared the toiling enemy, but still he came on in inexhaustible numbers.

I was called to Sergeant Eames, MM, of 'Charlie' Company, who lay dying on a forward slope amidst the burnt, blackened undergrowth. He was severely wounded, and death was in his eyes. I prayed with him as he requested, and comforted him as best I could. The doctor ran down to him for some minutes to check his condition, but was very quickly called to other cases. The RAMC Sergeant came and administered morphine. He too, was called away. I remained with Eames for some time longer. He had been a real friend, and I was loath to leave him. Fighting for breath, he commissioned me most earnestly to write to his mother and his young wife. Then he said, "Leave me, padre, leave me. Get back, think of your safety, leave me". The filmy eyes closed, the words ceased. I scrambled back to the medical aid post. No stretchers were available. There was a possibility of a blanket-carry if a blanket could be found. I was conscious of a great mental weariness: logical thought became difficult. On the enemy hill slope opposite I could see many little figures moving about among the bare trees.

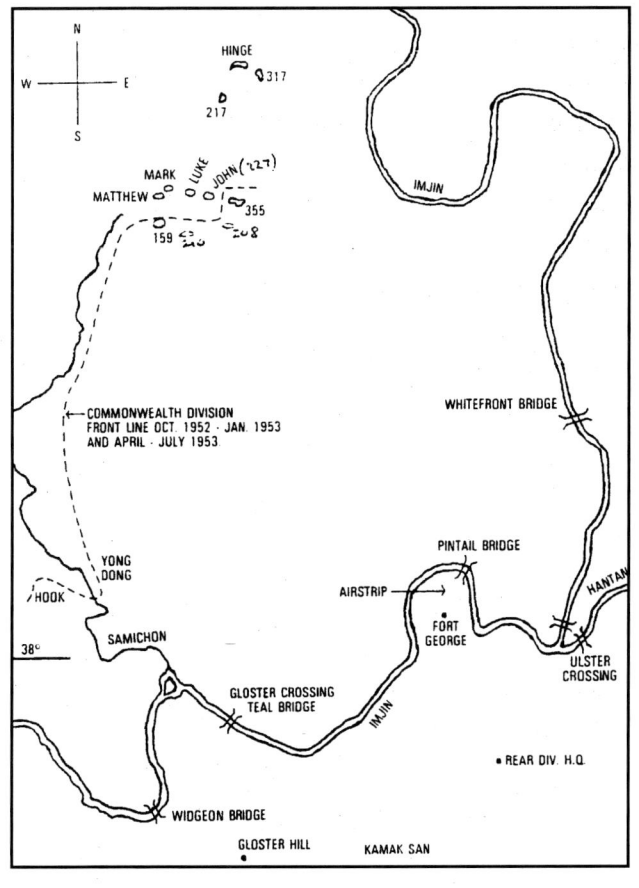

The Commonwealth Division area, 1951-53.

On my return to the aid post, I found the word had been passed that the Battalion would withdraw. No outside relief was possible. The guns, miles behind us, were themselves now under Chinese small-arms fire and compelled to fight their way out. They could no longer provide us with artillery support. Throughout the long engagement the Commanding Officers' coolness, determination and moral strength had sustained us all with a sense of confidence, and a spirit of resistance. The men had fought with a calm, stubborn bravery, not for a moment contemplating defeat. The Battalion had done all that could possibly be done; it was now no longer able to function effectively as a fighting unit. The order to withdraw was given; each company was to attempt a breakout of the Chinese encirclement as best it could. Sixteen miles of mountainous, enemy-infested country lay before the semi-exhausted troops. They began to pour off the fatal ridge in desperate but often jesting groups, disappearing into the deep, overgrown gullies. I urged especially the married men of the medical staff, along with my batman and driver, to make a run for it. I turned to the RAMC Sergeant. "This looks like a holiday in Peking for some of us", I said, smiling wanly. In a moment they were gone. Sergeant Brisland of the Gloucesters remained with me.

At this time the Medical Officer, Captain Bob Hickey, was forward at Battalion HQ, where he had been doing magnificent work for the wounded. He rejected any thought of flight, and remained 'til the end carrying on his great ministry. Bob and I had no contact at this critical moment, but independently of each other we immediately decided to remain behind on the ridge. It was a spontaneous decision, without heroics, clearly indicated by duty. Only when Colonel Carne was satisfied that his stricken men, whom it was impossible to evacuate, had someone to care for them did he leave the ridge in a gallant attempt to lead a fighting patrol back to the UN lines.

As I knelt there in the aid post by the side of a grey-faced wounded man, I saw Major 'Sam' Weller go down with his troops. He looked at me and shouted something. "Sam", I called out, "tell the Adjutant

I'm staying with the wounded". A few moments later Major Guy Ward scrambled down. Sergeant Brisland was preparing to wave a white Red Cross flag for the protection of the aid post when Drum-Major Buss suddenly appeared on his own, moustache bristling, in the now deserted weapon-pit above us. He clutched his rifle, shouting at Brisland: "Put that white flag down, you ... ". It was clear that 'Drummie' had not fully appreciated the situation. "The Battalion's gone, Drum-Major. For heaven's sake run for it, man – it's your only chance", I yelled. He looked at me with amazement, and then was gone down the slope.

Some yards above me, to the left of the weapon-pit, a 19 year old Gloucestershire lad lay dead, the vivid blood of youth welling from his mouth. I crawled up to him, and removed his rosary beads and letters. The letters I swiftly tore up, the beads I stuffed in my pocket. They were to remain with me throughout 2½ years of captivity. On my return to England I was able to give them to his parents.

A strange lull settled on the ridge. Some four or five able-bodied men stumbled into the aid post. I felt dazed, but not afraid. This seemed strange to me, because during the long battle I had known moments of acute fear. A mood of comparative nonchalance came over me. I looked along the ridge to the deserted ground held so gallantly by 'A' Company. A solitary grenade burst there. At any moment I expected to see Chinese troops surge over the crest. They did not do so. A sudden terror seized me lest British guns should start shelling the ridge. "If that happens, we've had it", I thought. But even this consideration failed to grip my tired mind with any permanence. I spoke to a man on a stretcher at my side. He too seemed calm and resigned.

Suddenly the first Chinese troops appeared above us, on the lip of the hollow in which the aid post lay; small, brown, extremely young-looking men. They were shabby and tattered, armed with new automatic weapons, and chattering excitedly. We raised our arms. Covering us with their weapons and shouting incomprehensibly, they motioned us to form in file. Bob Hickey, and the small group of prisoners with him, now joined us. We tried to demonstrate that we wished to carry our stretcher cases with us. But the Communist soldiers would brook no delay. We were marched down the mountainside, our palms on our heads. After a short distance we were allowed to help our walking wounded as best we could.

Through a South Korean interpreter, also taken prisoner, the doctor and I asked the Chinese officer at the foot of the hill whether we could return, under guard, and carry our stretcher-wounded down into the valley. His reply was, "No, do not fear. We, the Chinese Peoples' Volunteers, will bring your wounded down later". This promise was, I believe, carried out – so far as I can judge. Later that afternoon, the Chinese deprived Bob of his remaining instruments and medical kit.

The Chinese guards threw us a tin of Bully-beef and three loaves of bread (from our captured supply trucks), and brought water from a stream. This did not go far among some thirty-five of us, but it was our first food and drink, apart from a few biscuits in nearly forty-eight hours. All afternoon we lay, exhausted physically and mentally, in a tree covered gully looking across the small plain to the ground overlooking the Imjin. At about half past three, we saw the remnants of the battalion being led in under Chinese guards. The gallant bids at a break-through had, for the most part, failed. The two and a half weary years of captivity by the Chinese Communists had begun.

It was to be a long and stressful period in numerous camps. No contact with home, many dying of disease and injuries. It was to last until September 1953. Colonel Carne was to be awarded the Victoria Cross to add to his Distinguished Service Order, 'Sam' Davies gained a well-deserved; Member of the British Empire. He died on 15th March 2003 at the age of 91. Of the 2730 US servicemen who fell into enemy hands, 1096 died in Captivity and about 50 of the 1036 British prisoners failed to return.

'Sam', then records the long forced marches, wading the wide and fast running Imjin River, stripped of clothing and carrying the bundle over their heads, bitterly cold, without food or water, complete exhaustion, interrogated at 2am by young Chinese Officers who spoke very poor English. The problem he had was to convince them that he was a Priest. He had been given a list of ranks from General downwards and he was asked to point to the rank applicable to himself. He pointed to, 'Captain'. Another list appeared with trades. Transport Officer, Engineer, Artillery, but nothing which identified him as a Chaplain. He repeated over and over again that he was a Chaplain, Holy Christian teacher. The interrogator began to speak more sharply. "You are a Captain, you are with your Commander, Colonel Carne". It went on for hours. The party was addressed by a high ranking Officer who spoke stilted English:

> "Officers and soldiers of the British Army, you are now Prisoners of War of the Chinese Peoples Volunteer Forces in Korea. You have been duped by the American Imperialists. You are tools of the reactionary warmongers, fighting against the righteous cause of the Korean people, supported by their brothers, the Chinese people. You are hirelings of the barbarous, Syngman Rhee (President of South Korea) puppet government, but you will be given the chance to learn the truth through study, you will correct your mistakes. Do not be afraid, we will not harm you. At home your loved ones await you. Obey our rules and then we will not shoot you".

\* \* \* \* \* \*

Tony Eagles was a 22 year old soldier serving with the Gloucesters and captured with the Reverend 'Sam' Davies. It is horrifying and humbling and he is to be congratulated on his courage to overcome the cruelty he endured. This is his story:

We were on the march – 30 miles a night through the hills, and mostly keeping to the main roads as we were likely to be bombed by our own planes! We were the remnants of 29 Brigades RNFs, RURs,

Gloucesters, RA, 8 Kings Royal Irish Hussars etc. that had been captured on the Imjin River between 21st-25th April 1951 during the great Spring Offensive by the Chinese Army, and were now being marched to the POW Camps along the Yalu River which borders North Korea and China.

There were also a few Americans that we had picked up en route, and two of them came to where I was sitting with a group of young Drummers from the Gloucesters, accompanied by the large figure of Ron Allum of B Coy, Gloucesters. They suggested that I was apparently one of the fittest men in the Regiment, that I might listen to their plans to escape from the column and make our way to the coast, pick up a craft of some sort, and get into the China Sea off the West Coast of Korea, and hope to be picked up by a United Nations Forces ship patrolling the coast.

The two American soldiers had previously escaped and had been recaptured, but wished to try again. As I recall they were known as 'Blackie' and 'Davey', but I believe their actual names were Blackwell and Davies. I do not remember their ranks or units, but I understood they had been captured in November 1950 and had somehow survived the terrible winter despite being constantly on the move. They told me that a large number of their comrades had died of the severe cold, dysentery, malnutrition and other privations, and they were determined to escape again, even if it resulted in their death.

Our plans consisted solely of slipping silently from the column one by one, and meeting together when the column had gone past, bearing in mind that there were always one or two 'Tail-end Charlie's' bringing up the rear. Our signal to recognise each other would be an owl hoot, and if caught we would deny any collusion but insist that one had fallen ill and the other had stopped behind to assist him, and had met the others accidentally without knowing where we were going, and hoping to meet up with the rest of the prisoners.

That night, as we went along a narrow footpath in the hills, with plenty of shrubbery on either side, I slipped out of the column. The word was passed to Ron Allum, and he too slipped silently away, as did Blackie and Davey.

When I judged that the 'Tail-end Charlie's' had passed I gave a low hoot, answered by three hoots almost in unison. I called their names and they emerged from the shadows, each from a different direction, and moments later we were on our way.

It was a bright, starlit night as we set off in a Westerly direction, and we walked until dawn when we found a wooded place on some fairly high ground that gave us reasonable shelter, and here we rested for the day. We followed the same procedure for the next two days and nights, moving in a Westerly direction all the time. The morning of the fourth day found us in the hills in an ideal place amongst some trees. It was a very hot day and Blackie, Davey and I sought refuge in the shade from the blazing sun, but Ron insisted on lying in the sun, with the result that by the afternoon he became quite ill, presumably from mild sunstroke.

Although at our pre-escape talks we had agreed that should anyone of us become too ill to travel he would be left behind, when it happened we found we just could not leave a mate to the mercy of the elements, and God knows what else. I told Blackie and Davey that if they continued they would do so with our good wishes, but they declined and stated that we had started together, and we would sink or swim together.

We had a short council of war and decided that we needed water for Ron, and we would see what happened after that as the occasion rose. We moved down and across the hill until we arrived, quite suddenly, at a clearing in which was situated a house with a small courtyard and two outhouses. A small, elderly lady emerged from the house as we approached with some trepidation, looking much more nervous than we felt at that moment. Blackie and Davey had picked up a smattering of the language and explained that our comrade was ill and needed food and water. The old lady called to someone inside the house, and a few moments later an old Korean gentleman emerged and greeted us warmly.

The old lady spoke to him again and he indicated that we should enter the house quickly. Once inside they brought us drinking water, some boiled rice, meat and other vegetables which were spiced, and never was food better cooked or better tasting. The meal, however, did not include Kimchee, for which I found profoundly grateful, as I would have felt obliged to eat this very hot and spicy food, which I did not enjoy, and to this day will still have only a nominal taste.

After we had eaten, the lovely old Korean couple indicated that we were welcome to remain for a day or two in order to recover, and that night we slept well, taking it in turns to keep 'stag'. During the next two days, Ron Allum began to get better and take an interest in his surroundings. On the third day of our stay at about midday, the old lady came to our room very agitated and crying. It was obvious that something was very wrong.

It so happened that her 12 year old grandson had seen us and told his father of our presence in his grandparents' home. Realising that our discovery could imperil the safety of these two fine old people, we prepared to make a hasty retreat, but as we were giving our heartfelt thanks to them the boy and his father arrived, both armed with rifles.

We were made to stand in line on the veranda with me on the right and Blackie on the left. After a few moments they indicated that we should move off in single file, with the boy next to Blackie and the father next to me. It appeared to me that neither of them looked capable of handling their weapons, and I suggested to Blackie that it would be easy for us to disarm them, and that when I gave the word we should attack them simultaneously.

But before I could do so there came a burst of machine gun fire over our heads, and a Chinese soldier with about a dozen North Korean Police arrived.

We were then marched to the village nearby where Ron, who was obviously ill, was taken away by the Chinese soldier to his Headquarters, leaving the three of us at the mercy of the North Korean Police. They wasted no time in having some fun at our expense.

First they asked us our ages, and I told them that I was 22. Blackie and Davey both said they were 21, although in fact they were both older than me. They then bound our wrists together in front of us with electric cable, and ordered us to squat with our backs to the wall of the Police Station. One of them, who I took to be their leader, then lit a cigarette and offered it to me. I raised my head to take it when, without warning, he reversed it and pressed the burning end against my lips. I reacted quite angrily and spat in his face, a gesture which caused one of the other policemen to slam his rifle butt into my thigh with such force; I thought it must surely have been broken. Later I discovered that a cigarette case, which had been loaned to me by a Lance Corporal in the Royal Signals in Pusan, had been badly dented by the savagery of the blow. I still have that cigarette case.

We were then taken to the rear of the Police Station, and still bound, placed in a shed and ordered to squat, watched over by a guard. Sometime later a middle aged Korean entered carrying a stick about three feet in length and about 1½" thick with which he began to beat me about my head and shoulders in an apparent frenzy, his eyes blazing with hatred. I tried to dodge the blows as best I could, which was very difficult to do in a squatting position, and I truly thought he was going to beat me to death. With this thought uppermost in my mind I kicked out with all my strength, my right boot landing squarely in his crotch.

He doubled up screaming in agony, and I wondered if my action had been very wise. The guard, however, simply lifted him up and shoved him out of the shed. I discovered later that his home had been bombed and his entire family consisting of his wife, son, daughter-in-law and their four children had been killed.

Later on a man with an air of authority entered the shed and indicated to Blackie to follow him outside. Shortly afterwards we heard raised voices, amongst which we heard Blackie telling them in no uncertain manner what he thought of Kim Il Sung. Then we heard a number of shots.

Neither Davey nor I could say what was uppermost in our thoughts on the fate of Blackie, and sometime later this same man came back and beckoned to Davey to follow him. Davey looked at me and said, "Well Tony, I haven't known you long, but I've enjoyed your company. See you somewhere, sometime". He then followed the Korean out of the shed. Shortly after I heard several more shots, and I was convinced that both Blackie and Davey had been killed.

As I watched Davey leave I thought to myself, "That's it. I'm next". When you are faced with the prospect of imminent death under the circumstances in which I found myself, there is not a great deal that can be done about it, but I was certain that very shortly I too was going to be shot to death. With this thought uppermost in my mind I felt a sudden and pressing need to go to the toilet, which was situated outside the compound, and after asking permission of my guard, I was escorted there.

While I was there I saw two policemen walk over to a dugout and begin firing into it, and then I heard the voices of Blackie and Davey coming from inside, cursing the policemen, who appeared to be playing a game of sending ricochets around the dugout. At least they were still alive, but for how much longer I did not dare to think.

I was escorted back to the shed where I tried not to think of what was happening to my two comrades. A short while later they came for me.

As we left the shed, one of the Korean's said in broken English, "You Americans are criminals and do not deserve to live". I took great exception to this remark and retorted angrily, "If you are going to kill me then you had better know that I am not a Yank, but a British Soldier!"

At this, the Korean who had spoken to me said something very quickly to the others, and then turned to me and told me that if I was indeed English then it made a difference. I was then escorted back to the shed just as a platoon of Chinese soldiers arrived at the double. It seemed that they heard the firing and did not want the North Koreans killing their prisoners. They then marched Blackie, Davey and me to their Headquarters, where we were reunited with Ron, and given some food which consisted of what appeared to be chapattis filled with bean-shoots, which was very welcome and filling.

Later that night the four of us were marched away to our next destination. Ron was still unwell and after several hours wanted to give up, but I draped him over my shoulders and half carried, half dragged him along. After a while I began to tire, but refused to give up until I felt too exhausted to carry him any further. I began to perspire heavily, and my body began to itch all over. I looked up and saw that the moon, which was large and bright, and turned a vivid GREEN! Whatever it was that was wrong with me it was decidedly unpleasant, and shortly afterwards I became unconscious. I came round to find that Blackie and Davey were carrying me between them, and I shall always be grateful to them as the Chinese usually shot anyone who failed to keep up the pace.

Several days later, we arrived at a village which seemed to consist entirely of Chinese, and there our escorts handed us over. The man in charge appeared to be a Senior Officer whose face had been badly scarred by fire, probably during the Napalm attack. He was to be our interrogator and he began by separating us, and we did not see each other again until after our ordeal of interrogation was over.

One day I was taken into a courtyard where 'Scarface' was waiting, who indicated that I should sit down on a large boulder. He then proceeded to tell me that he knew me to be the ringleader who had organised our escape. I told him the story that we had agreed on when we planned our escape, but I could see by his expression that he did not believe me. He was carrying a Luger pistol which he then pointed at me, and said, "You are the ringleader".

I repeated that we had not planned the escape, at which reply he called to another man who had been standing nearby behind my right shoulder. This man had what I believed to be a British Army .38 revolver as issued to Officers, and making sure I saw what he was doing, he inserted one round into the otherwise empty chamber, and then spun it before placing the barrel to my head. 'Scarface' asked me again if I was the ringleader, and when I again denied it he nodded, and the man holding the revolver pulled the trigger!

I felt the click of the hammer to an empty chamber through the steel barrel resting against my forehead, but I was sufficiently well versed in the use of small arms to know that the weight of the round should ensure that it ought to be at the bottom when it ceased spinning. However, I did not know if the revolver was in good condition or not, and the thought that it might be faulty made me decidedly nervous.

The man holding the revolver now moved to my right side, and after spinning the chamber and allowing it to stop, once again pressed the barrel to my temple. The question was repeated, and I gave the same reply. 'Scarface' gave an order and again I heard the click, but this time it had a different sound, and my fear began to increase. I had heard of people getting killed playing 'Russian Roulette' and the thought suddenly flashed through my mind that suppose the bullet did not always drop to the bottom!

'Scarface' repeated the question, and this time I hesitated before replying, and with my hesitation came the realisation that 'Scarface' knew he had beaten me. The man with the revolver spun the chamber and pulled the trigger, but much more quickly this time, and then he moved behind me. I turned my head to see what he was doing, but was told to keep my eyes to the front. 'Scarface' gave an order and I heard the chamber being spun, and I suddenly thought, "What if he pulls the trigger before the chamber stops spinning!" It was not a pleasant thought.

Once again, 'Scarface' asked his question, and suddenly, now very afraid, I replied, "Yes, if you insist. I was the leader".

As I spoke I felt sick that I had been so afraid and had not stuck it out. I consoled myself with one thought that I could do more good alive than dead, providing I could outlive the punishment I knew I would get as a result of my confession.

Blackie and Davey were sentenced to 28 days in 'The Hole' as it was their second escape attempt. Ron and I received 14 days.

The 'Hole' was simply a hole in the ground that had a removable cover, through which we would crawl to answer the call of nature. On one occasion when I answering a call a sentry, who was on duty, dropped a bundle of tobacco leaves down to us. We still had a lighter and a small bible, the pages of which we used to roll our cigarettes, which helped to make those 14 days a little less disagreeable.

I often think about that lovely old Korean couple who helped us, and sincerely hope that they did not suffer for their actions. Given the circumstances they were probably punished, and I still feel guilty, and very sad about it. I trust that somewhere in their equivalent of Heaven they know that I truly appreciate, and remember, their kindness and courage in helping four Allied soldiers during the dark days of the Korean War.

# The 8th King's Royal Irish Hussars

8th King's Royal Irish Hussars evacuating
Northumbrian Fusiliers.

"They sailed to a foreign war in the name of decency and nothing else. Courageous, peaceable men of many nations met and fought as comrades, each under his own flag, on the field of honour, with an undivided purpose. They were to fight over a malodorous, nearly unheard of, Peninsular … defiantly, in a loathsome climate, against numerical and strategic odds that appeared to mock their weapons and military science". - "MEN OF VALOUR" … Part of the recorded history of The King's Royal Irish Hussars.

The 5th Royal Inniskilling Dragoon Guards have enjoyed a long and happy relationship with the 8th Hussars for many decades. It is based upon our Irish heritage and particularly the post Great War cuts in 1922 when Irish Cavalry regiments were amalgamated with English cavalry. In 1992 both regiments lost that identity and became The Royal Dragoon Guards and The Queen's Royal Hussars.

In the late forties, the 8th Hussars were withdrawn from the British Army of the Rhine (BAOR) to form a Brigade of Territorial Armoured Regiments, reforming in the Midlands. They were equipped with the Second World War main battle tank, the Cromwell.

When warned that they would form part of the United Nations force to re-enforce South Korea in November 1950 they not only had the problem of National Servicemen and aged regulars, but also to convert to the Centurion which was untried in battle. Reservists were recalled, some of them ex 'Skins'. Even the Medical Officer had been recalled. He was given a directive by his Commanding Officer that no officer was to be barred for medical reasons. This resulted in one officer with one leg and another having only one eye. At least they were rich in experience. The regiment fielded 48% reservists. The 29th Brigade was to include, the Gloucestershire Regiment, The Royal Ulster Rifles and the Northumberland Fusiliers. Some Cromwells were retained for their Reconnaissance Squadron. The Centurions were embarked straight from the manufacturers and therefore had not been run in; Korea was to be the testing ground. They had sailed from Southampton on 11 October 1950, on the Empire Fowey. The tanks were on separate ships. The lack of proper ramps to off load 52 ton tanks on arrival caused some delay; there was a similar problem in the northern terminus. They had to make a neutral turn and just drive off. One squadron set off to join troops on the front line but the South Koreans were already in full retreat. The Hussars were halted and joined the move south. The roads were hardly wide enough for a tank and refugees caused delays. During the drive, a tank ran over a South Korean soldier. His legs were crushed beneath the tank. A member of the crew dismounted to see what assistance could be given. A South

Korean officer immediately grabbed the crewman's revolver and shot the injured Korean. Anyone who hadn't already realised that this was not a conventional war suffered a nasty shock. It was probably the kindest thing to do in such circumstances. There was no way of evacuating the casualty quickly, nor any nearby hospital. The Korean officer would be unaware that tank First Aid boxes had both morphine and chloroform pads to deal with such problems.

'B'Squadron carrying men of the Royal Northumberland Fusiliers over the River Imjin during the advance of Lowther Force, April 1951.

The Hussars were most disappointed to have travelled 10,000 miles by sea and a further 200 miles by rail and road and not fired a shot. They had run the Centurions in and were satisfied with the mechanical performance, and they had firmly established that normal rules of war did not exist. The retreat was halted and there followed four months of heavy fighting to take them north of the Imjin River. They were to play a major role in the actions to rescue the isolated

## THE 8TH KINGS ROYAL IRISH HUSSARS

Gloucesters in the April 1951 battle. Captain Gavin Murray, a Second World War veteran, had volunteered from the 'Skins' and had already given a good account of himself during the preceding months. The following excerpts from the 8th Hussar history, 'Men of Valour' cover the period which led to his being awarded the Military Cross.

The 'Battle of the Imjin' has now been woven into the great tapestry of the 8th Hussars military past. It has confirmed the standards by which British soldiers in battle have been recognised through many centuries. The hard-fought fame of the Gloucester Battalion stands out, and has been justly honoured, above the rest, but our pride in them has been made warmer by the certainty that not only the Gloucesters, but any unit among us, would have stood fast and won the same high recognition, had the lot fallen otherwise. It was a time when each soldier, behind his more immediate thoughts and reactions, remembered how men had fought before in the British ranks, and felt the stronger sense of purpose from it. It must also be remembered that, in the first night and day of conflict, the Belgian Battalion, by their lonely and unfaltering action beyond the river, became more truly and integrally a part of our Brigade, than even those who knew and valued them most could anticipate.

The guns were firing over open sights at enemy on the hill, and Lieutenant Colonel Foster of the Fusiliers, rudely driven from his foxhole, had come back to Squadron Headquarters at 4am to ask for tank support. At a quarter past five, with barely light to steer by, three troops of tanks left leaguer under Captain G Murray, with the two tasks, one to support the Fusiliers counterattack to recapture the hill dominating the gun lines, and two, extricating 'Y' Company of the Fusiliers from their position in a northward loop of the river, which was now well forward of the precariously held line, but had been more or less ignored by the enveloping enemy force. Captain Murray, leaving one troop to assist in the counterattack, himself led the way into the threatened loop. Captain Murray was in immediate command of this operation, in which the tanks had to expose themselves on open ground, without Infantry protection, for two hours. By mid-morning a strong enemy force in possession of the dominating hill, Kamak San, was bringing fire to bear on the Gloucesters in the west, and also menacing the supply route down the valley behind the Northumberlands and Ulsters. The enemy now dominated all and occupied much of the high ground between the two main valleys, and with all his forces committed, Brigadier Brodie had no means of counterattacking. A re-disposition of the Centurion Troop in the east valley was therefore necessary. Murray was left holding the north of the valley with four Centurions and a Gunner Observer tank. The remaining troops were posted at tactical points down the road to keep it open at all costs. Lieutenant Venner and his Recce Patrol moved up and down the road between these points. Captain Murray picked out on the hillside what appeared to be some fresh bushes. He fired, and as many bushes as were able ran over the crest! He continued north. Radford in the leading troops came under very heavy, accurate mortar fire. The column was ordered to close down hatches and press on, but due to the lingering fog all periscopes were misted, and two tanks of three troops went off the road into the paddy. The first stopped, sensibly, and waited for a slackening of fire, but the second plunged into further difficulty by throwing both tracks. In the steep, rocky country, with no accompanying infantry, the tanks were open to close range attack and there were perhaps two hundred enemy in the area of this steep bend. One Chinaman leapt out from a ditch and threw a sticky bomb against the side of Radford's tank, it exploded, blowing a hole through the skirting plate, but leaving the suspension undamaged. Chinamen were now swarming among the rocks and bushes beside the road, but the closed-down tanks managed, by using inter-support machine-gun fire, to shoot them off each other's backs and turrets.

The tanks of Ormrod and Murray and four others, aided by Lieutenant Venner in his scout car, stood around, 'thrashing' the area with fire. Chinamen were crawling and scuttling for cover. Those who were able made their way into an irrigation ditch running down from the hills and in this way placed themselves out of reach. Despite the tremendous activity since dawn, it was still only a quarter to nine in the morning. Captain Ormrod described the danger spots on the road, which were now 'covered' by tanks, but under continuous threat. Lieutenant Boyall, with the Reserve Company of the Ulsters two miles back, had perched his tank on a startling eminence and obtained an admirable field of fire. He and his troop were in lively action against the Chinese visible on the foothills of the 'Kamak San', and so far had kept them at bay and the valley open at this point. But now they had reason to believe the road had been cut behind them. Just forward of this position and protected by a Sapper Troop. One of the bogged tanks was being recovered under a fluctuating volume of fire, with Captain Murray superintending. This effort, thanks to Murrays' sangfroid and determination was crowned with success. He was wounded several times in the course of the morning, but was not evacuated until the afternoon, when the last elements were pulling out.

# CITATION
## (2623) Captain G.S. Murray. 5 DG att 8H
### For The Military Cross

On 23rd April Capt. Murray was in command of the half C Squadron 8th Hussars which was ordered to extricate Y Company 1st Northumberland Fusiliers, after they had been cut off by the Chinese. This task was made difficult because the positions of our infantry were exposed to enemy fire. Captain Murray's coolness and personal leadership was greatly responsible for the success of the operation and the rescue of Y Company.

On 25th April this Officer was responsible for recovering one Centurion tank, which had thrown a track in full view of the enemy, and he was only beaten by time from recovering the second.

While he was out of his tank, directing not only recovery operations but also the evacuation of 1st Northumberland Fusiliers' wounded, he was firing his Bren gun at the approaching Chinese and this he continued to do till the last moment, in spite of being wounded in the head and shoulder.

# PREPARATION, A CALL TO ARM OURSELVES

In late June 1951 The 5th Royal Inniskilling Dragoon Guards assembled in the Camp Cinema, Barker Barracks, Paderborn, Germany, to learn that they would relieve the 8th Kings Royal Irish Hussars in Korea in the coming autumn.

As the Regiment left the cinema, small groups gathered to discuss problems. What would happen to the 80 families we had in the regiment? What about the National Servicemen (NSM), serving a 2 year compulsory tour? We had absorbed officers and men from other regiments which had been disbanded, particularly aged Warrant Officers. Some had not been with us during the war years and were physically too old. Those in positions responsible for clarification had much to do. The greatest concern was for the families. A ruling was made that any NSM would have to have at least a year to serve to qualify to accompany the regiment. Those who didn't qualify under this rule were given the option to change their National Service commitment to a regular period of three years. A high percentage took advantage of that. The family problem was a very difficult one. We had a large gathering of German wives and at least one each of Danish, French and Belgian nationalities. Some had never been to the UK before. The wives held a meeting and decided that they should all stick together whatever was decided. The great hope was that they would be accommodated in one of the requisitioned hotels in a seaside resort. This was a false hope. The offer was to be a Nissan hut in a disused Naval Camp in Corsham, Wiltshire. Some had no alternative and readily accepted, others decided to stick to the original plan and hope that something else would be offered. In August they set off for the UK escorted by the regimental band members who were to remain at a training depot in Catterick. The camp was awful. Run by a team awaiting demobilisation and untrained to cope with the many problems affecting their welfare. Schools for all ages, medical attention, and transport, all were problematical. It was too much for most and those who had an alternative took advantage of it. Some had to remain for eighteen months.

The Regiment was commanded by Lieutenant Colonel Arthur Carr, who had been a Prisoner of War from 1944 until the armistice in 1945. All but one of the squadrons was commanded by officers who had been drafted in, some were ex-regiment and the Warrant Officers and Sergeants had a similar mixed history. There had been five changes of Regimental Sergeant Majors and RSM George Chun, the appointed RSM had been serving with a Polish organisation since 1944. The junior NCOs were also from mixed backgrounds.

The reader might well believe that we were a regiment of some limitations. This was far from true. We had established a very well-bred stable which commenced with the confiscation of 3 Hamburg Police Horses. We had officers and men who could compete at international level and had been very successful in the many equitation events held throughout Germany. We had won the British Army of the Rhine Athletics Championship in 1950 and were a force to reckon with in a variety of sports. Advantage was taken to accommodate and make use of an Italian Fencing Master, and the Sports Master was a German who had been a 1936 Olympic discus thrower. We were very confident and were rated highly by other regiments. Above all, our gunnery reports were of the highest standard. Constant exercises to counter any Russian attempt to expand their empire had kept us well trained in armoured skills.

# PREPARATION, A CALL TO ARM OURSELVES

'A' Squadron.

# TRACKS IN KOREA

'B' Squadron.

# PREPARATION, A CALL TO ARM OURSELVES

'C' Squadron.

HQ Squadron.

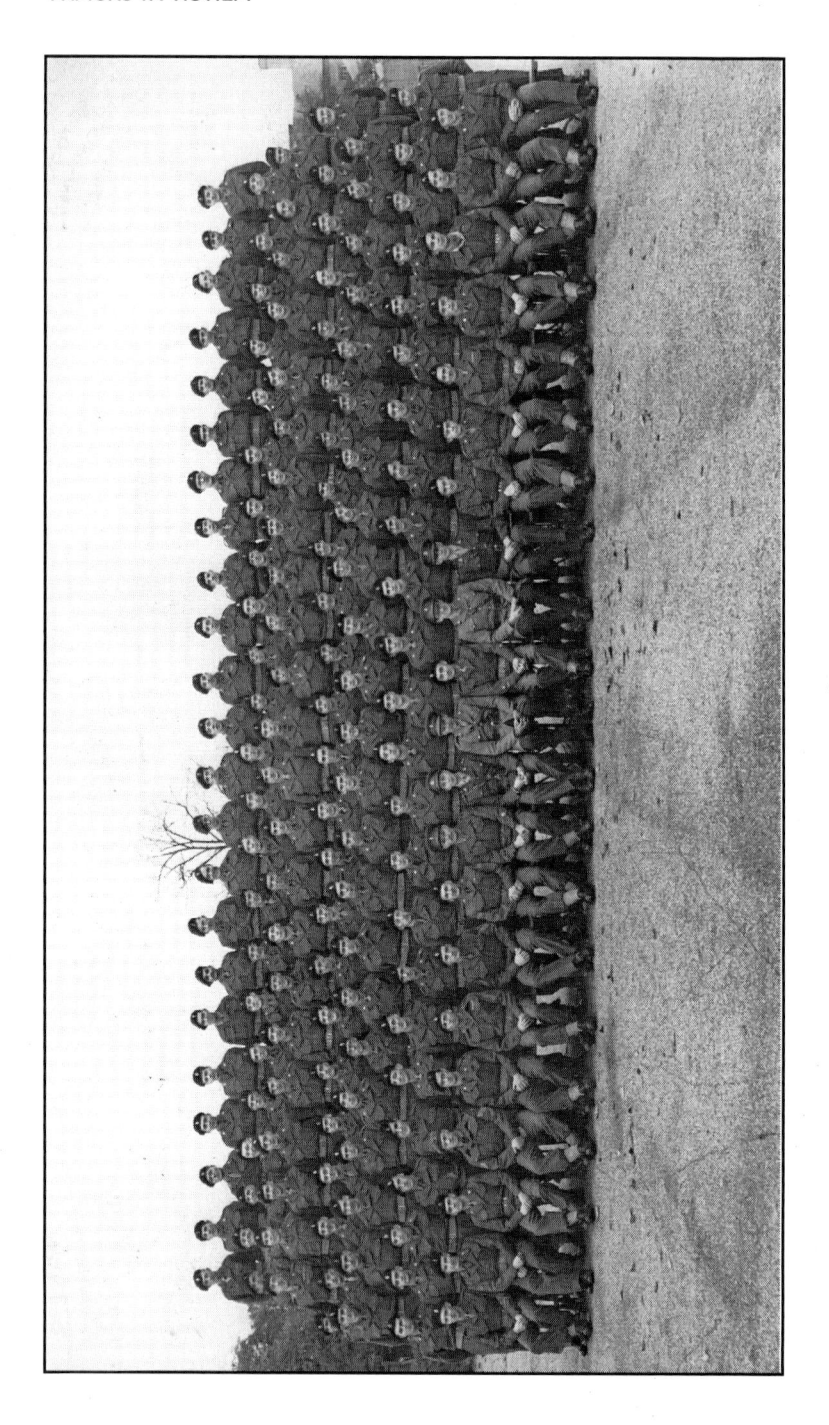

# PREPARATION, A CALL TO ARM OURSELVES

The Warrant Officers and Sergeants. RSM George Chun (centre)

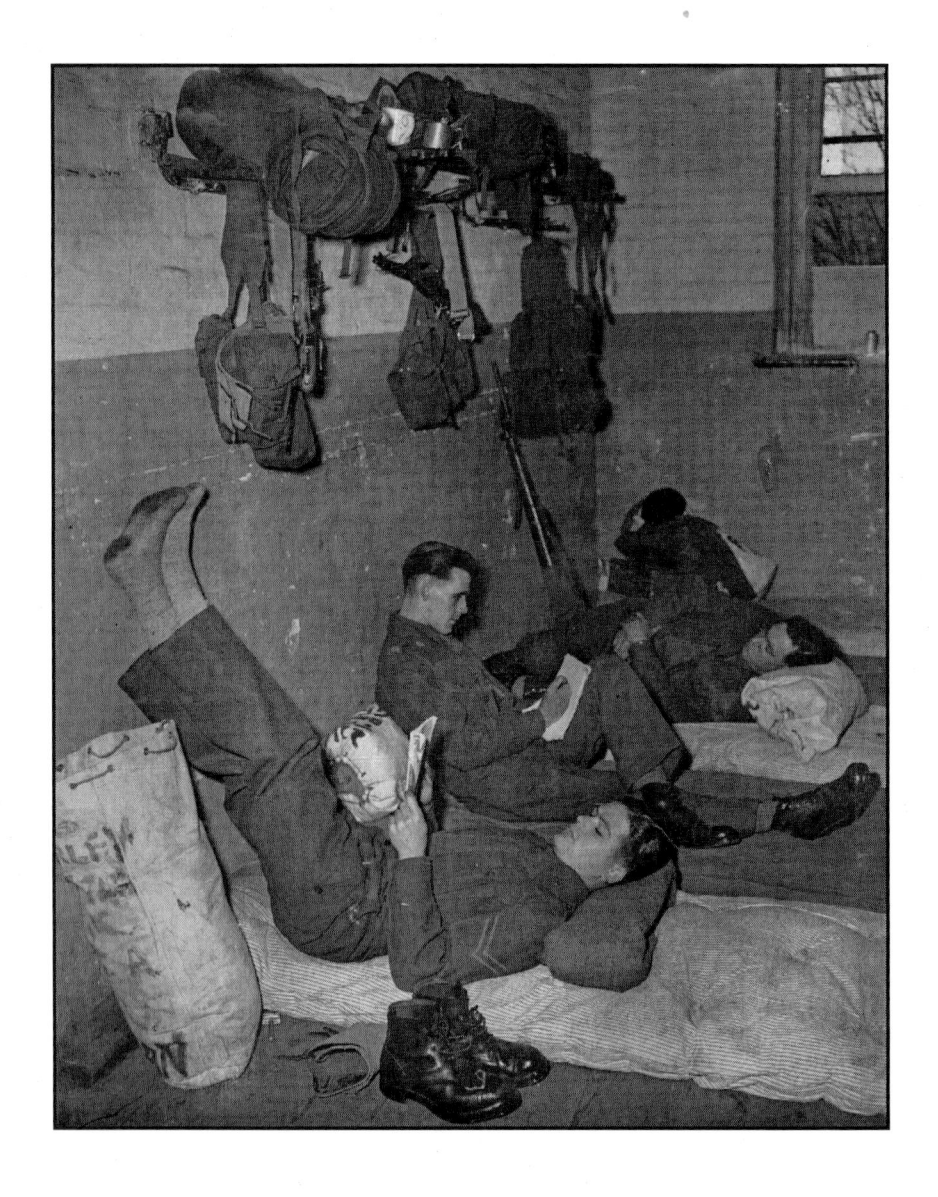

Awaiting Orders! Not a foot inspection: Aldershot.

## PREPARATION, A CALL TO ARM OURSELVES

Reports on conditions in Korea were arriving from the 8th Kings Royal Irish Hussars initiated by the few who had volunteered from the regiment to strengthen them, as we were having to do now. There were also men serving with the 8th who had been "Skins" before demobilisation but had been recalled to serve out their reserve period. They were to experience a difficult time because of the terrain, weather conditions, and the lack of any special clothing.

We departed from Germany in mid-September to take up residence in a barracks in Aldershot which had been the home of the 5th Royal Inniskilling Dragoon Guards many years earlier. Most departed immediately to take advantage of embarkation leave. On return there was a period of dental repairs and the issue of clothing we had never seen before; a very warm parka, with a hood which would lace up to leave a very small aperture for the mouth, combat jacket and trousers, thick gloves with an outer and inner, string vest to enable body heat to be retained, a pair of long john pants with a large split in the rear to avoid unnecessary exposure during the time of need. Finnish ski boots which had to be two sizes too large to permit two pairs of socks to be worn at the same time and a sleeping bag made of an outer, inner and liner. It was all very special. A white, sea kitbag to contain these items was also in the hand-out. Later when we arrived at Pusan, the Finnish ski boots were withdrawn and replaced with 'Boots, wet/cold'. These were wonderful. Leather with direct moulded rubber soles and complete with insoles.

A farewell parade and Church service in the Garrison Church, to lay up our Regimental Standard in the 5th Dragoon Guard Chapel, and we were ready to go. A few old comrades came to see us off and the 14/20th Hussars waved us off from Farnborough station with a volley of Thunder Flashes. We arrived at the Princess Landing Stage, Liverpool in the early morning to embark on the motor vessel 'Georgic', a ship of 51 thousand tons, which had been the transport for British emigrants travelling to Australia.

Laying up of the Regimental Standard. Brigadier H.O.Wiley acting Colonel of the Regiment takes the salute. Aldershot October 1951.

The band had arrived from Catterick where they were to remain during our absence and there was a gathering of friends from the Cheshire Yeomanry. A light incident came during the embarkation. 'C' Squadron, of which, I as a Squadron QM Sergeant had been detailed to join the baggage party to transfer kitbags to the hold of the ship. There was a long chain from the train to the gangway. After a short period a very smart Military Police Sergeant marched up to Major Harry Walker, made a perfect halt and said, "The Port Commandant's compliments Sir, all officers are to embark now". Harry Walker replied, "Sergeant, you may convey my compliments to the Port Commandant and inform him that my squadron is responsible for loading the ship". The Sergeant did an immaculate about turn and marched away. The loading continued. Five minutes later there was a repeat performance by the Police Sergeant who said, "The Port Commandant thanks you for your message but insists that all officers must embark now". I seldom ever saw Harry Walker lost for words and obviously having a problem in dealing with this annoying little man. He could not fault his turnout

## PREPARATION, A CALL TO ARM OURSELVES

or criticise his manner. He said, "What is your name Sergeant?" Reply; "Sergeant Smith Sir". "Give me your AB64 Part One", demanded Major Walker. The Sergeant, with a drill like movement went for his top left side pocket and withdrew the document as though he were fixing bayonet. The AB64 was a record of service and acted as identification. It had to be carried at all times. Harry thumbed through the pages and finding nothing to criticise, said, "You are overdue a TAB Inoculation, get it done". The Sergeant without a quiver thanked him, saluted, and marched away. This later led to Major Harry being prevented from boarding to say farewell. He was to fly ahead and meet us in Pusan. During all this our band had played almost non-stop and even after we were embarked, continued to play. In the late afternoon, Harry Vince, the Bandmaster permitted them to fall out and get refreshments. Almost immediately shore lines were untied and we sailed. As we cleared the gates of Liverpool Harbour we could hear from the dock the sound of our Regimental March, 'Fare Thee Well Inniskilling'.

# THE VOYAGE

In early October the advance party had departed, sailing from Southampton aboard the 'Empire Fowey' in company with 1st Battalion The Welsh Regiment. "Dressed very smartly in battle dress, '37 pattern belts, boots and anklets, all soldiers were then laid to attention in bunks whilst the inspecting officer from the local District HQ went his rounds before the ship sailed. In retrospect this and the voyage, although like a scene from Kipling, was a great experience. The normal troop-ship routine of lifeboat drills and the use of coloured discs for staggered meals in the troops' galley defeated those who tried to get two meals, except for a Royal Navy draft for the Far East Fleet whose pockets bulged with discs of every colour". The advance party disembarked at Pusan on 2nd November, and moved directly by train with the Welsh Regiment (and their goat mascot), reaching the 8th Hussars' areas on 4th November 1951.

*By Lieutenant Anthony Millen (later Brigadier)*

"We sailed from Liverpool on 29th October 1951 on board an ex White Star Liner, MV Georgic. The ship had a chequered history, having been sunk by enemy action in or near Suez during the war, and later raised. It had, I believe, the biggest diesel engines in the world! It was a wretched ship, built for the North Atlantic and therefore without air conditioning. Our forthcoming voyage was to be halfway round the world. The ports of call shown on the map bore many of the well-known names which made up the British Empire and were therefore full of romance and interest.

Almost every horizon we would cross had an Imperial outpost

# THE VOYAGE

nearby so that, despite getting ever further from home, we felt some pride in sailing where the sun never sets and where we assumed we would be in friendly territory. We were probably too young and politically naïve to appreciate that the days of Imperial Power and influence were numbered so that many familiar names and places would, all too soon, be removed from the pink atlas and become independent, and not always grateful, countries. At that time, a Union Jack would greet us at Gibraltar, Port Said and the Suez Canal, Aden, Colombo, Singapore and Hong Kong. How times have changed. Our passage through the Red Sea was very uncomfortable indeed. I was lucky to be placed in an outside cabin for only four, but eight less fortunate officers made the trip in an inside cabin known as 'The Snake Pit'. After the usual places, the Suez Canal, Aden, Ceylon, Singapore (where we were entertained by the C-in-C FARELF, General Sir Charles Keightley) and Hong Kong, we arrived in Pusan on 2nd December 1951 and were immediately engulfed by the appalling conditions of Korea. Its smells of putrefaction were overpowering despite the approaching winter. Our train, a windowless and freezing wonder, took us to the railhead at Toc-Chong.

******

**MARCONIGRAM**

EMPIREWINDRUSH — 18/11/1951. 0415

40.  18/11/1951.  0400.  OFFICERS FRANK.  GYSF.

To: COMMANDANT 5TH DRAGOONS GEORGIC.

FROM COMMANDANT EMPIREWINDRUSH UNDERSTOOD YOU ON EMPIREWINDRUSH STOP. PRESUMABLY YOUR MESSAGE NOT RECEIVED STOP THANK YOU STOP GOOD LUCK AND GOOD HUNTING STOP FROM ALL RANKS 4TH HUSSARS STOP AND FROM MYSELF.

SCOTTROYAL INNISKILLING FUSILIERS.

# TRACKS IN KOREA

M.V. Georgic.

### M.V. "GEORGIC"
Captain C. S. Williams

**The Schoolchildren aboard M.V. "Georgic" present**

## "NEVER TOO YOUNG"

### MONDAY, NOVEMBER 19th, 1951

Music from the Dance Band of 5 D G.
The Director, Lionel C. Ewers, introduces the Company.

1. Song — Pat White, Brian Dewhurst
   "Too Young"
2. Acrobatics — Jimmy White, Brian Dewhurst
   The Daredevils
3. Song — Pat White
   "Two Eyes are Blue"
4. Recital — Ann Rigby
   "The Lord of Tartary"
5. Song — Brian Dewhurst
   "There was an Old Nigger"
6. Recital — Angela Scarborough
   "Conra Dear"
7. Song — Pat White
   "Someone Like You"

INTERVAL
During which the Band will entertain you.

8. Song — Helen Ware
   "Good Luck, Good Health, God Bless You"
9. Banter — Ann Rigby and Roger Carter
   Do You Know?
10. Song — Brian Dewhurst
    "Silver Dollar"
11. Recital — Ethel Scofield
    "Lady Gwendoline"
12. Song — Pat White
    "The Bells of St. Mary's"
13. Acrobatics — Jimmy White, Brian Dewhurst
    The Daredevils
14. Finale — The Company
    "Now is the Hour"

THE KING
★

We are sure that all troops will join us in wishing the children
A HAPPY XMAS

Programme from children's pantomime aboard M.V. Georgic.

THE VOYAGE

SHORE PASS

H.T. GEORGIC

No. 322377. Rk. SQMS. Name BOARDMAN

Has permission to proceed ashore

at Colombo on 16 Nov. 51

from 1800 HRS to 2200 HRS

Capt,
Ship's Adjutant.


SHORE PASS

H.T. GEORGIC

No. 322377. Rk. SQMS Name BOARDMAN.

Has permission to proceed ashore

at Hong Kong on 27 Nov 51.

from 1400 to 2300

W F A Findlay
Capt.
Ship's Adjutant.

71

*Colonel Mike Anstice recalls as one of the subalterns in the 'Snake Pit'* it was only as troop deck orderly Officer when crossing the Bay of Biscay that I realised how privileged I was to have such accommodation. One of my tasks was to visit the troop decks late in the evening. On descending to deck level I was greeted by darkness, hammocks swinging in unison and an overpowering stink of vomit. I'm ashamed to say that I fled. For all of us it was a first visit east and the colour, noise and smells of the Crater Town in Aden were amazing. All shore visits in Colombo, Singapore and Hong Kong were a wonderful experience. I think we were all taken in by the various items for sale it including 'genuine' pearls and Parker Pens. Everything was such a contrast to post war Britain. Anchored in Pusan Harbour was a large hospital ship – a sign of reality. After the ghastly train journey we were collected and driven to our squadron lines – in our case reserve squadron – by 3 ton trucks. Mine driven by a large black man who assured me that his smashed windscreen was due to enemy fire. An unlikely story but at the time I was impressed, but tried not to show it. The handover was quick – the 8H troop leader told me that my .38 was useless and gave me his American 9mm carbine. I wish I still had it! Shortly after handover American deserters arrived offering to supplement our inadequate transport. We soon added some Jeeps to our fleet well-disguised as Commonwealth vehicles. One Jeep had Chaplain to the Forces written below the windscreen, and a brass gear stick knob. The price per Jeep was a few bottles of gin.

Editorial

The contradictory views of the standard of accommodation during the voyage can be linked to rank. Despite poor air circulation the difference in being in a bunk to being in a large area of hammocks was vast. I thought that it compared favourably with other trooping trips I had experienced and could have been far worse. A reminder came at Port Said. The journey had been uneventful and mostly out of sight of land.

# THE VOYAGE

Even Gibraltar was given a miss in darkness. Relationships with Egypt had been worsening since the end of the Second World War. A large ship full of troops, travelling ninety miles through a channel no wider than fifty yards in places could easily be a target. A destroyer led the convoy, followed by an aircraft-carrier, and another naval vessel to the rear. We were reissued with our personal weapons, told to keep out of sight but near Portholes. No doubt the Carrier had a complement of Marines on board. Apart from a lone Arab making rude gestures all was quiet through the miles of desert. At Kabrit, just south of the Great Bitter Lake, the band of the Royal Dragoons was playing but we had passed before any return of compliments could be made. Little did we guess that the following year we would be serving in this remote area. Clear of the Suez Canal we entered the Red Sea. Trooper 'Dicky' Bird suffered appendicitis and engines were stopped to permit the operation to be carried out.

There were families en route to Singapore and Hong Kong, mostly RAF and it was nice to see children playing. They kept very much to themselves until we were in the Red Sea and approaching Aden. The day before we docked, an RAF mother with three young daughters, aged three, seven and nine, approached me and asked whether I was going ashore. I hoped to because I wanted to buy a Christmas card and small presents for my own two children and get them into the military postal system. They had been informed that the families would not be permitted to go ashore unless accompanied by a male. I was of course delighted; it made a change from the male company I shared my days and nights with. Others were allocated families. From then on my surrogate daughters sought me out on a daily basis, particularly when their mother was coping with laundry, inoculations or other problems. I was lucky to have three girls to look after; others had boys who were constantly climbing up to lifeboats or doing other mischief. The children became linked to their temporary Dads. There was a repeat performance at Colombo, then Ceylon (now Sri Lanka). I was sorry when they left at Singapore. The mother wrote to me throughout our stay in Korea and the whole family met me when we docked en route for Egypt on the return voyage in December 1952.

After Aden we learned that the 19 set Radio was not efficient in the hills of Korea and that operators would have to revert to the Morse Code. This was probably because the 8$^{th}$ Hussars had a squadron detached. Practice keys were put aboard and I was warned that I might have to revert to my old trade as Wireless Instructor to revise the procedure.

On 2nd December the regiment disembarked at Pusan in clear sunny weather to the strains of 'big band jazz' played by American and Korean Military Bands. "The railway siding was some 1,000 yards away, and after six weeks aboard, with all the personal weapons and kit to carry, the distance might have been so many miles. Pusan, a sprawling port of shanty towns, was hideously overcrowded with thousands of refugees, while vast dumps of military stores and supplies lay on every side, through which large six-wheeled US Army trucks sped raising clouds of dust. The anchorage was crowded with shipping, and palls of smoke from Pusan's industry and power station hung in the still cold air over squalor, dust and an impression of disorganised chaos mingled with Eastern odours.

After two cold nights and the primitive discomforts of the troop train, whose rolling stock was of the '8 Chevaux/40 Hommes' variety, the regiment deeply appreciated the piping hot tea liberally laced with rum which the 8th Hussars provided at the Ui-jong-bu railhead north of Seoul early on 5th December. From here the squadrons moved to the forward reinforcement area of the Division for final briefing.

******

# THE VOYAGE

This book is specifically intended to record the experiences of the 5th Royal Inniskilling Dragoon Guards but it cannot be isolated from earlier battles which preceded our arrival. Hard lessons were learned from their experiences. Those regiments had been despatched at short notice without the specialist clothing which we enjoyed. They were to face an enemy familiar to the terrain and the extremes of climate, short in stature but very strong athletes. We all underestimated their ability in stealth and trained to attack in mass over open country and accept heavy losses. Indoctrinated in much the same way as suicide bombers of today operate, they could advance unseen, lay perfectly still for hours and strike at a time when it was considered safe. They were unpredictable. To add to the problems, the infantry short range radios did not work efficiently in hilly country and they depended upon a battery, a constant supply of which were necessary to cover 24 hours a day. The roads were narrow and usually with a sheer upward slope on one side and a sharp drop on the other. One vehicle broken down and in the case of a tank, unmoveable without another to tow or push it, completely blocked all advance to assist in a rescue or to permit a tactical retreat. Much of the technology included in the tank was of little use and, in the case of the Gloucesters' tragedy, restricted.

The coverage given in the 5th Royal Inniskilling Dragoon Guard's book, 'Change and Challenge' is, in my opinion, as good as we can get but by updating it and relating the on-going story there is great satisfaction for me. It has been a great honour, seldom afforded to an octogenarian.

# INTO BATTLE
### Extract from 'Change and Challenge'

All attempts to produce a complete nominal roll of all who served in Korea have failed because the 1951 Journal includes those who did not sail with us. Nor does it include those we inherited from the 8th Hussars or those who sailed but proceeded to Kure in Japan.

The regiment could field an exceptionally able team at many levels. The Commanding Officer was supported by Major Vigors as Second-in-Command, while Majors Monckton, Tomkin, Walker and Blundell-Brown led A, B, C and HQ Squadrons with brilliance, courage and panache. Captain Woods, who became Adjutant very early in 1952, was much assisted by RSM Chun while Captain (QM) Birchall, RQMS Green and TQMS Clarke were an exceptional team on the 'Q' side. The Warrant Officers and Sergeants provided a most skilled and widely experienced element, which went far to counterbalance the relative inexperience of the National Service junior NCOs and troopers.

Korea is a tough and very mountainous country with narrow, deep valleys patterned into small paddy fields divided by mud banks or 'bunds'. Towards the coast the valleys are broader and the hills less high, while the lower slopes have more millet fields. On the higher slopes inland scrub bushes and evergreens interspersed with rocks and boulders cover the hills, and a few stunted trees grow always downwind. In the smaller valleys, hamlets of thatched 'basha' roofs and mud walls lurked, joined by twisting footpaths. The main supply routes from Seoul and the network of earthen roads in the divisional area had been developed by the Sappers, (Royal Engineers) whose bulldozers, graders and dumper trucks were never idle.

While the summers were very hot, humid and wet, with

temperatures above 80°, the winters were cold and dry. Fierce blasts of icy wind, from the Polar region and Eastern Siberia blow from the north, and even in early December 10° of frost is normal at night. In early February 1952, 44° of frost was registered and a Headquarters operator's hand stuck to the tank when he forgot to put his gloves on before a Squadron "Net" at "Stand To". (A check in each radio's tuning). The tanks had to be started up every two hours at night but even so there was a constant demand for fresh batteries. In the early spring and late autumn at dawn the valleys were filled with mist while the tops of the hills and the mountains stood out darkly as in traditional Japanese prints.

Japan had wrested this country from the Chinese Empire over 200 years ago, and from Korea had mounted their assaults on Manchuria during the Russo-Japanese War of 1904-5 and in 1931. In 1945, after the surrender of Japan, and despite the hopes of the Western Allies, the country rapidly split into a Communist North Korea and Dr Syngman Rhee's semi-democratic South Korea, an uneasy truce being observed between them until 1950. In June of that year, tempted by the internal political and military weakness of South Korea, and the reduction to token strength of American forces in the Far East, North Korea invaded the South in the hope of achieving total victory so quickly that the world would accept the fait accompli.

When in the line, troops were deployed within infantry company localities all on the tops of the hills, and most crews lived beside their tanks, at first in tents and 'bashas', but later on all crews were in dugouts as the enemy shelling increased in scale. From these hilltop positions we had excellent fields of fire reaching deep into enemy territory. On 8th December when the last of the 8th Hussars had been relieved, 'C' Squadron were in the left forward brigade sector, while the Canadians held the right forward sector, and A and 'B' were in reserve, north and south of the River Imjin respectively. The forward troops stood to with their infantry comrades over the dawn period, and during the day cooked meals and carried out maintenance tasks in addition to shooting at any targets they could reach. The infantry were well aware of the accuracy of the 20-pounder gun combined with the excellent observation of the crew commander through his fire control peri-binoculars. On pin-point targets, the infantry correction was sometimes heard "about 18 inches to the right of your last shot". The tank commander's standard correction to his gunner was "Two puffs of wind right".

During the winter months, the hills being frozen as well as steep, the tanks could not easily change positions, and there were some problems about rotating tank crews in the more unpleasant company positions even when the infantry relief's took place once a fortnight. However, by the latter part of January 1952, B and 'A' Squadrons were deployed left and right respectively in the forward areas while 'C' Squadron had gone to reserve. Even two tanks of 'A' Squadron HQ were deployed in 'the playpen', an area unhealthy with sudden mortar bomb-bursts in the paddy east of the village of Un-Gol which lay in no man's land. Few of the tanks moving up to forward positions in the winter did so without casting a track. Crews soon became adept at breaking tracks with explosives, though Corporal Peacocke enthusiastically used a whole box at one go, and after the resulting major explosion a portion of the idler landed near the Commanding Officer some distance away. The Corporal was reduced to the ranks within an hour. An 'A' Squadron tank groaned its way up very steep slopes to a superb fire position on a small column between the very prominent hill features of Points 355 and 227. This feat of mountain mobility aroused high admiration among neighbouring American tank crews.

An armoured patrol by two tanks of 2nd Troop 'B' on 6 March roamed beyond our FDLs to Point 163 from which they engaged enemy positions. On the way back one tank (Sergeant Searle) overturned into a minefield, and after the uninjured crew and all removable stores and equipment had been recovered, the Sappers blew it up. The Oates Sunday Parade ten days later was the last regimental parade for Lieutenant Colonel Carr as Commanding Officer, and took place in bright sunshine beneath Gloucester Hill. As the other squadrons were busy, 'A' Squadron alone celebrated St Patrick's Day with a funfair and a basketball competition, but all squadrons were visited by the Colonel of The Regiment, General Sir Charles Keightley, who spent three days with the regiment from 26 March. On his arrival he was greeted by a regimental Guard of Honour of 48 NCOs and soldiers commanded by Captain WF Garnett. The Colonel indefatigably went everywhere, including forward tank positions, many of which were increasingly subjected to enemy shelling and mortaring. On 16th March, Lieutenant Critchley-Waring and Trooper Botterell (2nd Troop 'C' Squadron) suffered minor wounds.

While early April brought warmer weather, and the excellent winter clothing was handed in, the peace talks at Panmunjom drifted on interminably but inconclusively. RHQ Troop was placed under 'C' Squadron, who, using their Squadron Headquarters as another extra troop, deployed six troops in forward positions including one to cover the valley running westwards south of the company positions along the ridge from Point 210 to Point 159. RHQ Troop and 3rd Troop of the squadron assisted their neighbouring infantry in repulsing what was subsequently assessed as a battalion-size probe between Point 227 and Point 159 on the night of 5 April; the troops concerned fired nearly 400 HE rounds. Though on a greater scale, this was typical of many a night's activities.

Lieutenant Colonel Carr handed over to Lieutenant Colonel Vigors on 10th April, having been given very appropriately by the Warrant Officers and Sergeants a cigarette lighter in the shape of a model 'space-heater', the all-important stove by which every tent or dugout was warmed in Korea, and a '50 Gallon Drum' cigarette box from the Officers. The '50 Gallon Drum' in real life held the fuel for the space-heater and was mounted on tilted chocks outside the tent or dugout. All ranks knew how much Lieutenant Colonel Carr had achieved for the regiment in BAOR as well as Korea. He had raised the standards of administration very high in barracks or in the field, as well as our sporting reputation in Germany. In Korea he had speedily established good relations with commanders and senior staff officers especially over the raids in February. Lieutenant Colonel Vigors, having been Second-in-Command, was thoroughly au fait with all aspects of regimental life including the operational ones, and his assumption of command was very warmly welcomed by all ranks.

Meanwhile the operational tempo was heightening. Troops with the forward companies had a steadily more unpleasant time and spent longer by day and by night stood-to in their tanks. Larger fighting patrols on both sides sought to dominate no man's land and patrol planning and orders became more complex and detailed, the squadrons supporting these with success. The two most dangerous places were, not surprisingly, among the most prominent features in the forward defended localities, Point 159 and Point 355 whence we obtained excellent observation, the latter being known to our US allies as 'High Hell', or 'Little Gibraltar', because of its shape. 1st Troop 'B' on Point 355 was repeatedly shelled and mortared and on 5th May, Troopers Gardner, Gorman and Brown were wounded. More grievously, on 26th May '52, 122-mm shells crashed into the small area of 'A' Squadron Headquarters, killing Corporals' Brewer and Cook, wounding the Second-in-Command, Captain Duckworth, and three other men, as well as severely damaging bunkers, ammunition and petrol dumps.

Editorial

Wars are the breeding ground for sentimental poets. They are written from the heart, Rupert Brooke, 'Woodbine Willie', Kipling. No military book is complete without someone expressing feelings in verse.

INTO BATTLE

*Left:* Radio mechanic workshop A Sqdn 'sigs' November 1952 H.Q. troop.

*Below:*
Major Blundell-Brown HQ Sqdn

81

Hill 355 (Little Gibralter) and hill 227 (Chinese) on far left
8th November 1952.

Hull down(ish) opposite Hill 132
Lt. Mike Fane on turret.

INTO BATTLE

Lieutenants Anstice and Barnes.

Two A Sqdn. HQ soldiers at the 38th parallel.
October 1952.

Sgt George Howells, SSgt "Lofty" McCann, Sgt "Johnny" Irvine MM and SQMS Jim Boardman.

Hill 132.

INTO BATTLE

Bombing up.

Major Mike Tomkin MC, Captain Cuthbert REME
and Lieutenant Michael Anstice

Fording the Imjin.

'A' Squadron in a reserve position.

## INTO BATTLE

Making use of an eletric razor converted to 24v presented by Philips Electric. One per tank.

'Taffy Lewis' (right) with friends. Later he was seriously wounded during the Battle of The Hook.

A 'C' Squadron tank fording the Imjin.
Pintail Bridge is in the background.

A typical hilltop position.

# INTO BATTLE

Sgt Peacock shows off his Philips Electric Razor.

A 52 ton Centurion on the crest.

TRACKS IN KOREA

Crossing the river Imjin May 1952.

'A' Sqn, 'Bashers'.

# INTO BATTLE

Hill 355 in Winter 1952.

3rd troop 'A' Sqn. in reserve December 1952.

A view of hill 227 from hill 228.

'A' squadron fitters.

Cfn. Pearson in his tank suit.

A dug out. Note the space heater on the left and sten gun.

1st troop 'A' Squadron in reserve position
Dececember 1951.

210 trench system. January 1952.

# INTO BATTLE

'B' Squadron waiting for orders.

'B' Squadron movong up.

'A' Squadron tank on hill 355 June 1952.

Hull down (i.e. tracks below skyline) on hill 208 December 1952.

'A' squadron tank in position.

On hill 159. November 1952.

TRACKS IN KOREA

3rd troop in reserve 'A' Squadron. December 1952.

On hill 208. Tank names 'Artist Glory',
one of a number given the names of fmous racehorses.

# Poem by Craftsman DA Pearson
*(A member of the 'A' Squadron fitters who kept our vehicles battle-worthy, often having to repair them under difficult circumstances.)*

We landed in Korea on a bright and sunny day
The Yanks had brought a band out to play us on our way
We thought – well this don't seem too bad in spite of what's been said
But of course we did not know the things that really lay ahead
A day in Pusan's Transit Camp, then on the move again
This time much faster, we had to take the train
We had seating made of wood, like park benches, for example
Toc-Chong railhead, reached at last
We all suffered from the journey
Next stop the numbered hills no less
With all the noise and smoke and stress
But no, we had just one more stop
Before the final hop
The RHQ and HAD, a hive of much activity (Heavy Aid Detachment)
A rat hunt, fast and furious, was going on just then
I should have made a note of it, but I hadn't got a pen
Entrenching tools, spades and such
All wielded with malignant touch
Spellbound, we stood and watched with awe
A rat race never seen before
Then that same day, down from the line, came a Trooper, killed on 159
This was his first stop on the way
To Pusan where so many lay

# TRACKS IN KOREA

He'd only got three weeks to do
Before demob and home was due
But fate again did take a hand
He'd be left forever in a foreign land
Then on my own up with the rations
To 208, supporting so many Nations
Within the range of Chinese mortars
Hutches in the hill for quarters
The one I shared with Jock and Scouse
Bore no relation to a house
We'd dug it out by hand you see
But with a bit of help from the ARV (Armoured Recovery Vehicle)
The infantry were out in front
And they're the ones who bore the brunt
Of hostile probes and sometimes more
When trying for an even score
With bugle calls and yells and screams
Enough to make you have bad dreams
The tanks, though in supporting role
Also had to pay a toll
In blood and guts encased in steel
But time marched on with no respite
From summers' green, the hills turned white
And then at last there came the day
The 1st Tanks came, hip, hip, hooray
Toc-Chon railhead, once again
Back on that bloody train
Nine and twenty hours it took
There was plenty of time to read a book
'War and Peace', just to mention
Down to Pusan, no more tension
No more frozen hands and eyelids
And also no more slides and skids

POEM BY Cft. D. A. PEARSON

Next stop Shandur – sun and sand
Not far from the Promised Land
Though better than the cold of late
The bullshit posed another hate
Unit smokers were quite good
Lots of beer and Toxon food  (Toxon , a Korean word for plenty)
Tea dances down in Fayid were had
All in all life not too bad
But all good things must end one day
Time to pack and sail away
With time expired and duty done
It's time to jack it in Old Son.

TRACKS IN KOREA

The train from Pusan to C-Chon

Jack Clayton, Rob Roy (drum major) Black Watch and TQMS Nobby Clarke.

# OPERATIONS LIVERPOOL, JEHU AND ASCOT

The Black Watch pipes and drums entertaining the regiment.
8th December 1952.

# OPERATIONS LIVERPOOL, JEHU AND ASCOT

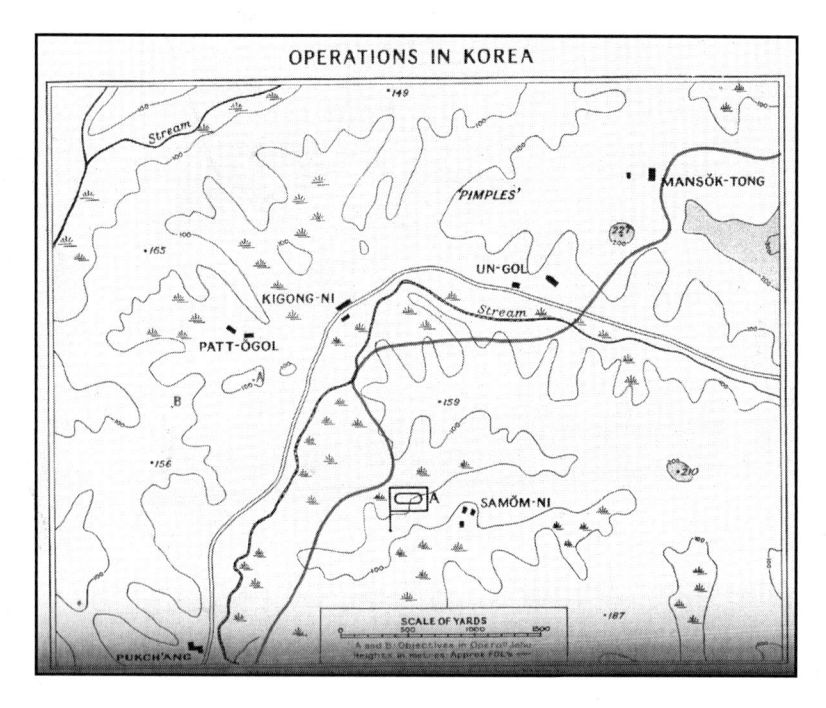

Covering Operations Liverpool, Jehu and Maindy.

*Change and Challenge,*

**The UN Command** tried to lure the enemy into assaults in the open, where our defensive firepower and air-forces could wreak havoc. The first phase was to reduce all movement to a minimum and to ban radio communications in order to suggest that our forward troops had been thinned out. The second phase involved two distinct but related

## OPERATIONS, LIVERPOOL, JEHU AND ASCOT

armoured raids by the regiment simulating a minor offensive during which it was hoped enemy artillery positions would be disclosed. Operation Liverpool, under 28th Brigade, involved the regiment less 'B' Squadron, supported by 3rd Royal Australian Regiment and 16th Field Regiment RNZA. Operation ASCOT, under 29th Brigade, concerned 'B' Squadron, supported by 1st Leicesters and 14th Field Regiment RA.

The detailed plan for Liverpool specified that 'C' Squadron less two troops, covered by 'A' Squadron and artillery fire were to advance west to Un-Gol, a village beyond our FDLs in the valley, establish themselves on the 'Pimples' feature of the Chinese-held ridge to the north and if possible exploit north and north-east in order to bring fire to bear on the reverse enemy-held slope of Point 227. In Operation ASCOT, one troop of 'B' was ordered to seize 'Mile End', a feature beyond the Samichon River, covered by the rest of the Squadron. The 'going' in area was understood to be less good. For Liverpool RHQ was to be on Point 210 beside the Brigade Commander's observation post, and 'B' Leader would control Ascot from Point 122.

At 06.30 hours on 16th February, the artillery and the infantry mortars opened fire, but the morning was still too dark for the tanks to move over the tricky ground, and both operations were delayed for 15 minutes. The Liverpool operation eventually got underway at 06.45 hours with 'C' Squadron 'Tug' (a turret-less Centurion used for personnel, stores and recovery), carrying a section of Royal Engineers to breach our own minefields, followed by 3rd Troop, 'C' Squadron HQ and the Artillery Forward Observation Officer, and then by 2nd Troop. Progress was delayed at first by the friendly minefield clearance, and the Sapper subaltern was mortally wounded by fragments of a mine set off by the 'Tug'. After 40 minutes, 3rd Troop was able to advance on Un-Gol, but shortly afterwards the leading tank was halted by an anti-tank mine which broke the track and damaged two road wheels. The Sappers came forward again and cleared the track into and through the village. By 08.30 hours, 3rd Troop, 2nd Troop, and Squadron HQ were past Un-Gol and struggling up the steep slopes to the 'Pimples', codenamed 'Matthew' and 'Mark'. Under constant sniping and mortar fire, and over rough steep going, progress was very slow, despite heavy fire support from 'A' Squadron, Lieutenant Findlay (3rd Troop) was wounded, suffering flash burns round the eyes. 2nd Troop (Lieutenant DP Rowat) on the right, faced similar difficulties but progressed slowly up from Un-Gol. Meanwhile the tank of the Squadron Leader (Major Walker) had shed a track at the base of the hill and 'in full view of the enemy he sat on the turret of his tank imperturbably directing the squadron … a marvellous example to those in their first mobile battle.

Regimental Headquarters
CO's Conference March 1952.
L-R Lt. Col A Carr, Major HC Walker MC, Major G Blundell-Brown, Captain HG Woods MC, Major RC de Vigors DSO, Major GR Monkton MC.

TAC HQ MAY, 1952.

*Sergeant 'Don' Pooley*

Early on 17th June, the Sappers breached our own anti-personnel minefields and wire, and by 0500, 1st Troop 'B' Squadron had moved down the valley between Points 210 and 227 towards Un-Gol as a diversion to suggest another Operation Liverpool and to engage targets on Point 165, i.e. to the west of their position and north-east of the main objective, but without any enemy reaction. At 0500, 1st Troop 'C' Squadron crossed the start line while prearranged supporting tank fire broke down the 'bund' beyond the stream in the valley between them and the objective. "Led by Lieutenant Taylor, fresh from an infantry patrol over this area, the troop went at a fine gallop and soon established itself on the first objective, a 100 metre high ridge half way to the main objective". Behind them heavy enemy artillery fire poured down on the troops of 'A' Squadron from Russian-made 122-mm guns. "The passage of 1st Troop across the paddy had broken the 'bunds', and now the area rapidly turned into a quagmire". Three tanks were soon bogged, the Artillery FOO, 4 (Troop Leader) and 4A (Troop Sergeant).

1st Troop was now told to push on to the final objective still covered by 'A' Squadron and also by 'C' Squadron HQ and the remaining tank of 4th Troop, all of which had reached the first objective. The advance was renewed an hour later and all was going well when Lieutenant Taylor's tank was hit by either a 'bazooka' or a projectile from a recoilless rifle. "The turret was not pierced but a small fire was started. This was put out by Taylor who dismounted to do so". A few Chinamen had been seen before they dived like rabbits into their trenches and bunkers, from which they sniped at the tanks. 1A destroyed a mountain gun which had opened fire at close range and Sergeant Bertrand wrote, "I found myself running up a fairly narrow spur with a long enemy communication trench dangerously near the tank track, and to cap it all, the danger of a bunker collapsing under the weight of a 52-ton Centurion was also a possibility".

1st Troop was soon within 100 yards of the final objective, but unable to surmount the rocky spur on the crest. They were, however, able to fire at bunkers not normally seen from our own lines, and one shot revealed an enormous bunker almost on the crest, which immediately received the full attention of 'A' Squadron and the Divisional Artillery. At 0630, the Commanding Officer gave the order to withdraw, which meant for 1st Troop and the Squadron Leader's tank, damaged by a 'Schumine' and exhibiting strong symptoms of engine trouble, a perilous return to our own lines. The route out through the minefield had been unfortunately blocked by a tank minus its tracks, thus necessitating a return over the face of Point 159 at a speed of about 3mph and through another of our own minefields; this of course delighted the enemy guns, who for what seemed like hours to the tank crews involved, had good targets to engage. The Chinese infantry now emerged from their bunkers and opened up with small arms, while their artillery poured over 100 rounds into RHQ and 'A' Squadron HQ in an hour and a half. SSM Clayton's tank was hit four times and all 'marvelled at his debonair unconcern in leaving his lid open; only the exercise of considerable restraint kept him from going over to

## OPERATIONS, LIVERPOOL, JEHU AND ASCOT

personally 'inspect' the opposition'. Within an hour the raiding force were safely back within our forward area, except for the tanks stuck in the valley below. For the offensive spirit he displayed throughout Operation JEHU, Lieutenant Taylor was awarded the Military Cross.

The problem of the three bogged tanks still had to be solved and the first Armoured Recovery Vehicle (ARV) sent out went over a mine which displaced its engine so that it joined the others. As RHQ and 'A' Squadron HQ pulled back, the enemy's artillery turned their fire on to the remaining obvious target – 'the four tanks in a bog being shelled'. A second ARV went out, and as it moved forward its winch rope was cut by a shell. Captain Cuthbert, the Electrical and Mechanical Engineer, was wounded whilst directing recovery operations dismounted. The 'Tug' with the medical team aboard set forth and it also got bogged, bringing the score to 'five in the mire being shelled'. With a great deal of hard work under fire, which however mercifully slackened, three out of the five were recovered by the end of the day.

The subsequent recovery of the remaining tank and the mined ARV became an operation in itself. On 19th June the Sappers cleared another route through our own minefields west of Point 159 and bulldozed a new track alongside the paddy. On 20th June the Technical Adjutant, Captain Cupper, led two patched-up ARVs in a 'Tug' to the mined ARV. The recovery group came under enemy mortar fire, but a pre-arranged smoke screen programme was called for, which the New Zealand gunners maintained for three hours. When the ARV was pulled over Point 159, and the smoke screen began to clear, the Chinese artillery again opened up vigorously. On Point 159, Second Lieutenant A Albrecht (4th Troop 'A' Squadron) was killed, his tank set on fire, and both Captain Manning (Second Captain 'A' Squadron) and our New Zealand Forward Observation Officer were wounded.

The Divisional Commander (Major General Cassels) directed that the remaining bogged tank (4th Troop Leader 'C' Squadron) be left in the paddy for another week. The final recovery operation was delayed by the first rains, involved ARVs and 'Tugs' under Captain Cupper, and took four days. Support for this tricky Commonwealth operation was co-ordinated by the Second-in-Command (Major Monckton) as Australian infantry patrols covered the tank by night, British Sappers assisted by day, and New Zealand gunners again laid smoke screens. Despite aftermath problems, Jehu was an undoubted success, as damage was done to the enemy's defences and he reacted afterwards by digging large anti-tank ditches.

******

Mr Montgomery-Hyde MP for Belfast with Major GWR Monkton.

*Sergeant 'Don' Pooley's account*

As reported elsewhere progress was slow due to the rough steep terrain and near the base of the hill the Squadron Leader's tank, shed a track. I was the Squadron Leader's operator; Corporal David McGill was the driver and Corporal Tom Carlyon, the gunner.

It soon became apparent that we had a problem with one of the tracks. With Major Walker's agreement Cpl McGill and I dismounted from the tank to investigate. Unlike today's modern army, we had no body or head protection and were under some small arms fire. The left track had jumped off the front idler wheel and jammed between the idler wheel and the hull. We tried to free it but the tension at that time between the jammed track and the drive sprocket at the rear was too great. We then decided to try and break the track by removing a track pin at ground level. Due to the tension this proved impossible. The decision then was to blow the track. We had on board explosive charges for this very purpose. The 8th Hussars had handed over these explosives to us at the take-over. However we had not had any training in the use of them. (This possibly explains why Corporal Peacocke was a little enthusiastic with the use of the explosive in attempting to break a track). Corporal McGill and I duly packed the charge on the track adjacent to the drive sprocket at ground level. The net result was like a damp squib, so again failure in breaking the track. Whilst all this was going on Major Walker remained with his head and shoulders out of the top of the turret directing fire from the rest of the squadron. He also had the additional task of maintaining contact with RHQ on our second 19 set tuned into the RHQ frequency. Cpl McGill and I resorted to brute force using crowbars to lever the track off the idler wheel. We were successful and able to slacken the idler wheel and get the track relocated. After some skilful driving we finally adjusted the tension and were ready to go. I have no idea how long this all took, but it did seem an eternity. Shortly after getting back into the tank the order came to withdraw. We slowly reversed down the hill and returned to our reserve location. Our thanks had to go to those supporting tanks whose fire kept the Chinese infantry in their bunkers preventing them from using small arms fire against us whilst the track was repaired.

Though 'C' Squadron were firm on their objective by 1130, exploitation over the crest and to the rear of Point 227 was not practicable without infantry to clear bunkers. At 12.30, withdrawal was ordered, and the tanks began to pull out. "As the Chinese realised what was afoot their fire from automatic weapons and mortars increased and they came up from the depths of their bunkers". 2nd Troop's Sergeant received an anti-tank high explosive shot from a suspected recoilless gun, making a three and a half inch hole in the turret, luckily without damage to tank or crew. By 14.00, and under heavy covering fire, all were back within our lines, and the grey winter's afternoon was no longer punctuated by the smoke and dust of many shell and mortar bursts. In the midst of the operation the message "Hullo 17A it's a boy, over" puzzled many on the radio net, except Major Monckton in 'A' Squadron HQ, who thus learnt that he was a proud father.

Unfortunately, on the left Ascot went less well. The going was very sticky and treacherous, the route lying along the steep frozen south slopes of Point 163. Later the surface thawed, and the tanks slipped and slithered over the frozen subsoil, finally shedding tracks. By 12.00, it was obvious that no amount of effort would get them to 'Mile End', and, withdrawal having been ordered, 2nd Troop 'B' returned slowly and safely to our own lines.

The regiment earned much praise from senior commanders and other Arms after the raids, in which the courage and professional skills of all ranks had been so amply demonstrated.

*Trooper Fred Towns-Mason relates*

The 26 May 1952, just another day at 'A' Squadron. The troops with the forward companies had been busier of late, but for us, we just grumbled and carried on regardless. We were paraded for our duties to be allocated by SSM Jack Clayton. As we waited, we were aware of enemy artillery rumbling and the shells they were firing getting ever closer. Then just as 'Jack' was approaching us with our instructions a salvo screamed in and exploded amongst the bunkers and ammo dumps at the bottom of our re-entry. We scattered. Two of us dived into a cut-away in the hillside where we just looked at each other. I remarked upon my friend's white face, whereupon he said, "not half as white as yours mate!" At that moment we heard SSM Clayton yelling for some of us to get down to where the mayhem was and do something useful. We ran down and found quite a few people milling around. Someone came out of a bunker that had been hit holding a book with a large piece of shrapnel still stuck in it. At that moment another salvo of 122mm shells landed amongst us. Everyone again dived for cover. John Holman and I went in different directions. I threw myself into a small, very small slit-trench nearby, which although not very deep, had some 20-pounder shell containers as head cover. Not being of Military Medal material I dived in head first, landing with my face in the dirt and my legs still exposed. I quickly righted myself, spat out a mouthful of sand and cowered for all I was worth. Another of the many salvoes of shells arrived, convincing me that my hideaway was unsafe, without more ado I scrambled out and made for the Centurion Tug which was a few yards away. I intended to get under the back end of it. Unfortunately, or more likely very fortunately for me, the space was occupied and I was told to f... off to the other end, which I did with haste. I crawled in under the Tug where I noted that I now knew where John Holman had gone. Others under the Tug were 'Terry' Reynolds, 'Ron' Brewer and Brian Cook, RNZAC attached. More shells landed in the small area of 'A' Squadron, which was only about 45 yards by 75 yards wide, and most of them seemed to be landing in the lower 100 yards, we were all startled when one exploded so close that shrapnel or stones were blasted between the road wheels. At this 'Ron' Brewer shouted for all of us to keep our mouths open, this was to equalise the pressure or something. I shouted back that as far as I was concerned I should have stayed in my slit-trench. He answered, "Don't be daft; you are as safe as anywhere under this Tug". Within seconds, our world was torn apart. For my part it was as if I had been punched in the face. My vision was one of a red hell: then, oblivion. I don't remember anything more until I came to in the advanced aid station, with a doctor cutting my shirt up the front. I wondered why he wasn't undoing the buttons. It turned out that I had enough blood over my face and shirt for him to believe I was badly wounded. This was not the case; all I had was a small piece of stone sticking out of my left pectoral muscle. The blood had obviously been blasted over me from 'Ron' Brewer and Brian Cook, although I was unaware at this time of their fate. I again remember nothing until I woke up a few days later in the Psychiatric ward in the 25th or 28th Canadian Field Hospital, where I spent a couple of weeks. I was told I was being sent back to the UK but managed to persuade them to send me back the HQ Squadron. Later I learned that my younger brother, John was coming out with the 1st Royal Tank Regiment to relieve us, so I made a request to claim him to the 'Skins'. I was told that if I could find someone who would prefer to do another year in Korea, rather than go to Shandur Egypt, it would be okay. As it turned out I think most of us would rather have stayed in Korea than serve in the dump called Shandur! One day in Shandur, I was sitting on my bed talking with my brother when a terrific bang just outside the tent sent me into shock. I do remember someone, a Scot, remonstrating with the culprit, a Captain Martel, who had discharged a shotgun at some piehard dogs. (wild dogs). Again I came- to in hospital (Fayid). They shipped me back to 'Blighty' to Netley Military Hospital and eventual discharge.

Editorial

There were other heroes in this action, particularly Sergeant John Newport, who did a wonderful job in treating the wounded while himself under attack. Medical officers stated later that no-one could have done more. He was awarded a Mention in Despatches but many agreed that he deserved a higher commendation.

Captain Peter Duckworth was acting as Squadron Leader when the attack was made. He left the command tank and ran down the hill to assess the damage. He assisted where he could then ran up the hill to re-join his tank and make reports. During this short journey he was struck above the eyes, probably by flying stones and was unaware of the blood on his clothing. He was later evacuated.

*Sergeant Don Pooley adds:*

In mid-June it was decided that the regiment should carry out an armoured raid somewhere on the Divisional front before the rainy season, due any day after 21st June. The force was 'C' Squadron less two troops, with two infantry sections of 1st Princess Patricia's Canadian Light Infantry and a Sapper detachment under command, and two 'Tugs', whilst in addition, a medical 'Tug' and two ARVs were to be on call in the Assembly Area. The Commanding Officer selected as the objective the Point 156 feature and the spur just to the north of it, which was believed to be a battalion position, with several enemy mortars suspected on its reverse slope. A few tracked vehicles (either tanks or SPs) had been seen occasionally in this area, and little was known of enemy dispositions which in any case might have altered after a recent formation relief. The main aim of 'Operation Jehu' was to raid Point 156 and inflict maximum damage on the enemy. It was also hoped to obtain a prisoner for identification. 'A' Squadron, with under command 1st Troop 'B' and a troop of The Lord Strathcona's Horse, which latter troops were already deployed, were to give tank fire support, while the whole Divisional Artillery, the mortars of the 1st Battalion PPCLI and the medium machine-gun section of the 1st Battalion Royal Leicester Regiment were also available. We, together with 4th Troop, were in support of 1st Troop who were trying to reach the objective. During the approach we had to negotiate paddy fields, which had been churned up by 1st Troop. 4th Troop lost two tanks bogged down but some skilful driving kept us going. It was at this point that I heard two loud bangs in fairly quick succession. The second one I felt had come from the underside of the tank at the rear end. Corporal McGill realised that something had happened but kept the tank going. We later discovered we had detonated two Schumines whilst bellying through the paddy field. The first one detonated at the front end of the tank inflicting little damage. The second had detonated under the gearbox, damaging the mounting supports and cracking the gearbox causing an oil leak. When the order to withdraw was given Corporal McGill was experiencing considerable problems engaging gears. He was only able to maintain bottom gear as we struggled back to our own lines.

\* \* \* \* \* \*

The day before the raid some of 'A' Squadron Troop Leaders and crew commanders were carrying out the reconnaissance of their special fire positions in support of Jehu. For one troop to lose all its crew commanders even before the battle is joined was a shattering experience, but an anti-personnel mine seriously wounded 2nd Troop Leader (Second Lieutenant Sutherland), and less grievously his other tank commanders. Mr Sutherland lost a foot.

\* \* \* \* \* \*

*Mrs Jan Fisher,* daughter of the late John Kinch, dedicated this story in memory of her father, who had related it to her. In her covering letter she told of a nervous interview on her local radio station as part of the 2010 Remembrance Service. "I did it for my Dad". She said, "My Dad served his National Service from 1951 till 1953, but all of us who knew him might have thought he had been in the army all his life"

Cfn. Tpr. Oxley, L/Cpl. Norris, Sgt. Pearson, L/Cpl. Glover

*Tanks Across The Paddy Fields - Trooper John Kinch*

As an 18 year old National Serviceman, in 1951, I was shipped overseas to experience active service, driving a Centurion tank, facing the enemy in the hills and valleys of the treacherous paddy fields of North Korea. That is why, on 9th July 2003, I was in London for the commemoration parade and service celebrating the fiftieth anniversary of the end of hostilities in Korea. It was a very special occasion and for me it turned out to be even more memorable.

At Horse Guards Parade, early in the day, I met Pete Williamson, a tank commander who I had not seen for over 50 years. He asked me how I had recognised him. He had not a hair on his head and he was wearing glasses now, but I recognised the gap in his teeth – that hadn't changed! After the parade and the service in Westminster Abbey, we took a taxi to The Royal Chelsea Hospital and over the luncheon we reminisced, particularly about the day that we both remembered so well – the day when we lost our commanders in one blow ...

A big raid, code-named 'Operation Jehu', was planned for the 17th June. 1952. It was to attack Point 156 to inflict maximum damage on the enemy. It was hoped we would capture a prisoner for identification. The day before the raid some of 'A' Squadron troop leaders and crew commanders were carrying out the reconnaissance of the special fire positions. We were ordered to leave our safe-haven and tackle the valley in front of us.

Lieutenant 'Fergie' Sutherland said to me, "You see that ridge half a mile ahead in no man's land, I want you to drive to the foot of that and make a track for the other tanks to follow, without getting bogged down in the paddy fields. Stop there and if nothing happens the rest of the tanks will follow". He went on, "Trooper Kinch, if you get there without losing a track I'll give you 10 shillings, I bet you can't do it". I replied, "Right, you're on".

So away we went. My mate, our radio operator, 'Ron', was a Mario Lanza fan. I can remember how we sang all the way down the valley, driving with the hatches open and waiting to see if the enemy would fire. The other tanks waited and watched.

When we reached our destination, just below the ridge, we stopped. I had managed it without losing a track. The other three tanks then followed our path. While we dismounted and started brewing up, we radioed back to base to say everything was okay and that no-one had fired on us, Lieutenant Sutherland said to the other commanders – Sergeant McCready, Sergeant Love and Sergeant Osborne, "Come with me, we're going up to the top of the ridge". It had been mined but our sappers had cleared it, or so they thought. So up they went on foot, we were all going there on the next day to support the attack that was planned.

Suddenly there was the sound of an explosion. We stared up to the skyline and saw 'Drew' McCready silhouetted against the evening sky, waving his arms and yelling for medical help. Someone had trodden on a mine! Without time to think of our own safety we rushed up the hillside to give whatever help we could. What a sight met our eyes. We found them all stretched out. The Corporal was wounded in the eyes, Sergeant McCready was wounded in the back, and Lieutenant Sutherland was lying on the floor in agony with a horrible leg injury. As I lifted him I could see how badly hurt he was. Stretchers arrived and all Sutherland could say was; "Get the bubbly out of my tank", so one of the boys went down to find his bottle of wine and brought it to him. We carried the wounded men down a bit of a path to our starting point and handed them over to the infantry medical staff that had arrived. They carried them back.

By then it was dusk and there we were, left on our own with no commanders. It was a very unusual situation. Eventually, new commanders arrived.

As I was carrying 'Fergie' Sutherland back I had looked at him and thought to myself – although I couldn't say it under the circumstances, "You bet me I would lose a track off my tank going down that valley, now you've lost one of yours!" It was a horrible thought but it did flash through my mind!

Fifty years later when attending the 50th Memorial Service, we were going over this story, when another person sitting nearby, who I think was an ex-colonel said, "I've been listening to your story. That fellow you're talking about is sitting over there. Do you want to meet him?"

He took me over and I met Lieutenant 'Fergie' Sutherland and we had a great reunion. In the course of our conversation I said jokingly, "Do you remember that bet you made, that I'd lose a track? The ten bob must have earned a lot of interest by now!" Of course I wasn't serious.

Anyway, after a lot of talk we said our goodbyes. That was that. It was great to meet him again and hear that he was well and living in Southern Ireland. In fact that wasn't the end, a week or so later a lovely letter came to me from him enclosing a cheque for £100!

I felt that it really did complete a very memorable story. It was donated to the MS Society and the Fund for Deaf Children. Jan's granddaughter was given the name Imogen because the River Imjin had been mentioned so many times by John.

(Footnote: Sadly, Fergie Sutherland died during the writing of this book).

******

*The late Captain Ian Manning became a casualty as a result of the attack on Hill 159 and gave his account in the 1952 Regimental Journal. It is typical of the combined sharing of resources which was so appreciated. Ian doesn't disclose the nature of his injuries but I can report that it caused him some discomfort in a sitting position. Read on:*

# A STUFFED FISH IN A GLASS CASE

KOREA TO KURE—AND RETURN
or
A STUFFED FISH IN A GLASS CASE

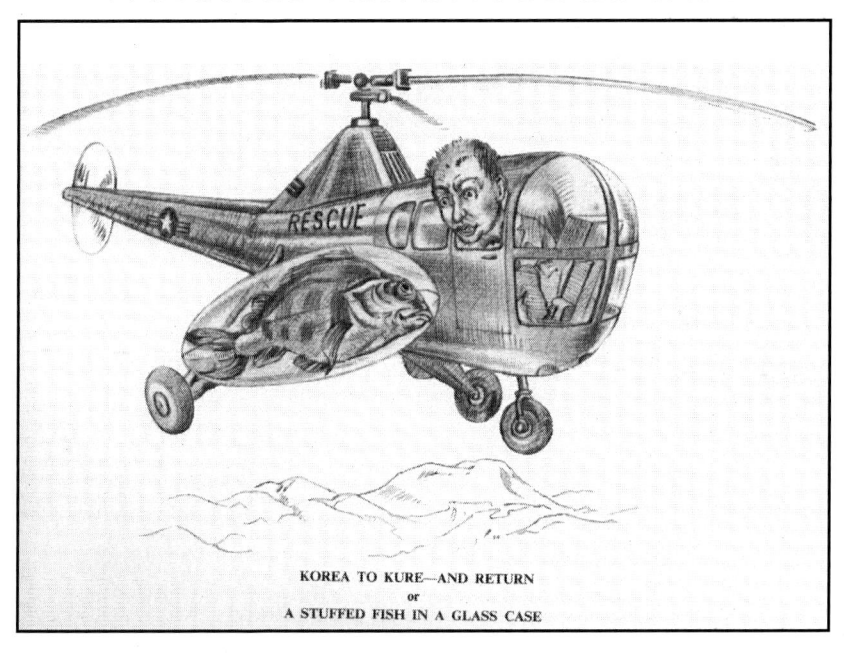

There is no doubt that, taken on the whole, the best method of travel today is neither the British Railways nor the Jaguar XK 120, nor the all-conquering USS "United States," nor yet the Comet Airliner. It is the helicopter. Especially is this so when its flight succeeds a bumpy, dusty ride in an ambulance jeep from a hill which most of the Commonwealth Division, past and present, know well as Hill 159.

Perhaps we might follow the progress of the individual who has been wounded by a Chinese shell on Hill 159:

121

First, he is tended by a stretcher-bearer of let us say, "D" Company of the 1st Bn The Royal Australian Regiment, who performed a minimum of first aid – mainly consisting of removing the patient's clothes – and then assists him to one of the dug-outs. Here he undergoes further immediate treatment which in this case consists of the removal of his boots, being bandaged with field dressings and having a drink of brandy. Having rested there for a while, he is helped from the dug-out, wrapped in a blanket, laid on a stretcher and taken to the Company Aid Post, a little farther down the hill. Shortly afterwards the ambulance jeep arrives and transports him to the Regimental Aid Post. It is no fault of the driver or his assistant that this journey is rough: the discomfort itself is offset by the knowledge that the enemy's shells are swiftly left behind.

The Regimental Aid Post is very strongly built and seems to be well equipped with supplies. It is also well, though ominously, provisioned with padres, who are kind and helpful. Now also the Medical Officer takes a hand, but no treatment is necessary, except the first of an interminable series of injections. Soon after, with a minimum of personal possessions, hurriedly brought down from Squadron Headquarters in a small bag, the casualty is loaded on to the helicopter, where he relaxes inside a Perspex container (US helicopters were fitted with container on each side, the British having no helicopters at this time), feeling like a stuffed fish in a glass case. This is a new sensation, to say the least. Life takes on a different aspect; the impersonal style can no longer be sustained.

So the helicopter left the ground with a rushing of winds, but with scarcely any other indication of movement. After a very comfortable journey southwards, during which the Korean hills appeared from a new angle, the machine landed, as gently as a cat, outside an American hospital north of Seoul. I was carried on the stretcher, still naked under the blanket, still clutching my small bag, into a large tent. My documents were completed and these, together with seven X-ray photographs, accompanied me throughout the rest of the journey. Following more injections and blood tests, some colourless liquid was dripped into my arm. I think blood had been intended, but, since this was patently unnecessary, I was given water, in the hope that I might not be disappointed. This is admittedly, only a theory.

Here also I had my first experience of "Pentothal", a wonderful drug indeed, since it induces sleep in the most agreeable manner possible. I awoke some hours later, but soon slept again. I spent the night in this hospital and was visited by several members of the Regiment, including the padre and the doctor, but doubt whether I showed much intelligence.

The following day I was conveyed by train to another American hospital at Yongdongpo, and, on arrival, was deposited in the entrance hall which was a vast stone affair, while the attendants wandered off to join what sounded like a premature Fourth of July celebration along the passage. In this institution, I achieved a shave and was visited by the American Red Cross and the American Chaplains' Department, which presented me respectively with a tube of toothpaste and a religious booklet, both free of charge. The next day I went by air to Iwakuni, on the Japanese coast. At this stage, the party became all Commonwealth. The aircraft was flown by Australians and had Australian attendants, one being female. The passengers included Australians, New Zealanders and Canadians, not to mention English, Scots and Welsh. After a comfortable journey, we spent some fifteen minutes at the Australian hospital at Iwakuni, where we had a meal, and finished the journey by train. On Sunday evening, two and a half days after leaving Point 159, I was in Bed 7 in Ward 11 at 29 British Commonwealth General Hospital in Kure, being tended by an English nursing sister.

Once there, I soon settled comfortably into the rut of hospital life. Some extraordinary events occurred of course – such as being moved first to Bed 3, then to Bed 2, then to Bed 29. There were the visits to the theatre (operating), which were in no way distressing (except that we had no breakfast), because, having started with an injection, we would travel on a trolley to the anaesthetist's room, feeling pleasantly drowsy and well-disposed towards all. There followed an injection of Pentothal, which unfortunately seems to live up to the name by which it is known to the layman, namely, the "Truth Drug". On these occasions, the orderlies invariably and hopefully wheel in an oxygen cylinder, which would stand in the corner of the ward against the returning victim, who should presumably be gasping like an expiring fish. I never saw it used or needed.

We often saw Father John Ryan, whom most members of the Regiment knew in Germany. There was also a pleasant Canadian, who gave broadcasts on a station so pleasantly named "Britcom." Perhaps, however, it was "the small padre", who buckled down to his job with the greatest energy. He had a long talk with us one morning, in which he told us of all the bad cases (physically) which he had seen during the preceding six months. "Poor chap," we thought, "he needs cheering up". But, nothing daunted and against all opposition, he pushed on to objective, which was apparently summarized in the remark. "You see, you could easily be worse off. There are others in a worse way than you". Since at the time of his advent I had been lying comfortably in bed reading "Men Only," I was not disposed to argue.

A further event which enlightened the inevitable boredom of hospital life was the visit of the Colonel and Major Tomkin. The high point of the three-day stay in Kure, as far as we were concerned was the miraculous production of an excellent meal, which we ate a little furtively, but very gladly in the reading room at the end of the passage.

In the beginning, the factors which governed our existence were fairly simple. There was the daily attempted avoidance of the bed bath, which consists, as you may know, of being rubbed all over with a slimy sponge or furtive flannel by two RAMC privates. These hide the patient behind bed screens, ostensibly to protect the patient's modesty. Then there was the thrill of guessing which of its limited selection of gramophone records the "Britcom" would play next (though it was always "Wheel of Fortune" – indeed, it is being played now). There was also the all-important question as to whether all the egg sandwiches would be eaten before the plate reached us at tea-time. This, incidentally, followed the tradition of hospitals by being at 3 o'clock.

Later, when we had won emancipation from bed-baths and similar loathsome amenities, we took a greater interest in what went on around us. We would begin to consider getting up and going into Kure town, which is just down the road and has a fair shopping centre. We would wonder about a place called Miya-Jima, which was apparently a leave and convalescent centre on an island in the Inland Sea. We would consider the roster of sisters working on the ward, which seemed to change at incredibly short intervals. Then we were introduced to physiotherapy – toe-waggling, electric currents and the rest. Then, at last, we found ourselves on the train to Miya-Jima.

Miya-Jima is a Japanese holy island, with a great floating shrine, a holy horse, holy deer and masses of not very holy looking ducks. There are also numbers of average holy Japanese, not to mention the Commonwealth element. The shrine is not genuinely floating, in that it rests on wooden piles, buried in the mud, which are exposed at low tide. The convalescent centre was run by NCOs and a Japanese domestic staff. It was never necessary to wear uniform and one was entirely relieved of any consideration for rank, either of oneself or of anyone else, other than in the normal way of courtesy. Indeed, there was a Padre Lieutenant-Colonel there for a week whom I for some reason confused with a junior officer in the Merchant Navy. Our main occupations were swimming and rowing in the Inland Sea (very warm and salty, but in places, rather dirty), and eating, drinking and sleeping. We lived in a requisitioned hotel, the accommodation and service being excellent. The food was taken from Australian Army rations and was not very thrilling, but one could feed well at a hotel in the village.

A further point of interest, especially to the officers, was the constant flow of sisters and nurses from the hospital. During my period there, we met English, Scottish, Australian and Canadian girls, most of whom we had known in uniform. These were either on a well-earned rest after two weeks night duty, or were taking their normal R&R

leave. I, for one, welcomed their presence except when it came to the "bathroom". Delighted to find that I had drawn a room with a bath adjoining, I had been accustomed to use this bath without reserve or undue modesty. One day, I discovered that a French Canadian girl was doing the same. We met. There was a hurried gathering of towels and a wordless departure through opposing doors. It transpired that she shared the room in the far side of the bath with another sister and that the bathroom itself could no longer be regarded as my property. On the departure of these two, the room was again occupied by women, so that careful reconnaissance remained essential at all times. Incidentally, I shared a room with a gunner who, at no time (particularly in the morning) required of me either intelligent talk or sensible listening. The room was intended for rest and for rest it was used. Indeed, I always took my breakfast in bed and did not hurry to leave it.

In addition to the normal run of life at Miya-Jima, there were various excitements, such as water pistols and fire crackers, both of which novelties seemed to be the prerogatives of the British officer and the Japanese child. The water pistol period culminated in my room companion spraying blue-black ink into the right eye of a Canadian Public Relations Officer at a close range. The highlight of the cracker game was the positioning of four crackers in an original and most dangerous position under a particular kind of seat.

Then there was Sukiyaki.

One night, three of us went down to the chief hotel in the village and, in order to learn how the natives lived, ordered Sukiyaki. Having discarded our shoes at the entrance, in favour of Japanese slippers, we were led by a Mamma-san (woman) to an upstairs room, where we were required to squat on cushions around a low table with a hole in the centre. It was a hot night, soon made hotter by the introduction into the hole of a stove bowl, shaped like an inverted top hat, containing burning charcoal. Next arrived in quick succession, a large dish of food, a shallow metal basin, chopsticks and sake. The basin was fitted over the fire and the cooking started. As pieces of food were cooked, we removed them from the centre with chopstick, with no little difficulty, and put them in small bowls which had been placed in front of us. In each of these we had broken and whipped a raw egg. We then ate cross-legged (until relaxing into a sprawl) a meal consisting of the following items; small slices of beef steak (the main ingredient), onions, some unknown vegetable which looked like tangled brown string, and some square off-white lumps of something which resembled yeast. The whole was mixed with soya sauce, a little hot water and mounds of sugar. We ate all this with chopsticks. For myself it was much too sweet and taken in conjunction with sake, a drink which seems to equal in potency a normal white wine, the whole effect was somewhat unusual. Sake, which is drunk at about blood heat, is served in small narrow-necked china bottles. It is distilled from rice and is colourless. It is drunk from a shallow cup the size of a liqueur glass, and appears to have no ill effects on the health.

While we were consuming this exotic meal upstairs, the normal Japanese, in their inscrutable manner (if people can be inscrutable who never seem to stop talking or, indeed, yapping) were sitting around tables in the restaurant below, wielding knives and forks over such unusual Eastern delicacies as steak and chips, ham omelette and chicken Maryland. I resolved, in future, to emulate them.

But I was persuaded again - I cannot remember why – and spent a memorable evening in the company of an English Red Cross sister, the Canadian Public Relations Officer, an officer of the Royal Canadian Horse Artillery, a Canadian padre and an officer of the Royal Army Pay Corps. The meal followed the usual pattern, though we achieved two platefuls of rice at about half-way. In addition, the management was determined on one of two courses of action; either to direct the first two members of the party to a separate room or to bring us up to strength with the issue of a girl-san apiece. We stood firm and averted both threats, but, as a tribute to our increased numbers, two mamma-sans came to serve us.

It was then that I discovered the Japanese method of drinking sake. If someone fills your cup you must drink the contents in one, refill it and hand it to the originator, who repeats the performance. The difficulty will be apparent, in that, if mamma-san is partial to sake and selects you as her favoured victim, there is no stopping. In this case, the result was most unexpected, for the younger Japanese girl became seriously affected by a passion which caused her to pinch, with unexampled ferocity, the fleshy parts of anyone within reach. She was finally restrained, none too soon, and we paid the bill and left. The food on this occasion was quite agreeable, as the sugar content was ruthlessly restricted. However, having drunk only sake all evening, a very thirsty night ensued.

A few days later, the period at Miya-Jima ended. We found ourselves, at half-past seven on a bright Thursday morning seated in a motor launch on the return journey to Kure. We arrived at the hospital bronzed and comparatively fit, to find the place much the same as ever. After an X-ray examination, I was instructed to report to the Convalescent Depot which stood beside a quay in the dock area of Kure. It is run by the Royal Army Medical Corps (RAMC), with the assistance of the Army Physical Training Corps (APTC). In the beginning, I was one of two officer inmates. In a well-staffed mess, with excellent cooking, we found life most agreeable. At the end of a further two weeks we were to return to the regiment by air. It is really the end of the story. But before I close let me join together a few loose ends.

Generally speaking, I have described the progress of any member of the Commonwealth Division from the time of being wounded to the time of his return to his unit. Regardless of rank, there are few differences. I must, however, report a major tragedy which affects our successors. One morning the Convalescent Depot Officers Mess was invaded by seven officers in varying dress, who appeared on first reports to have burnt Miya-Jima. What, in fact, had happened was that the previous afternoon the hotel at Miya-Jima had been ignited by an unknown agency and burnt to the ground, together with a great deal of personal and public property.

Finally, I will say some words about the hospital. The treatment we received was, I regret to say, invariably taken for granted. While this is a mark of gross ingratitude, it must also be recognised as a deserved tribute to the surgeons, nursing sisters and medical orderlies and members of the Red Cross, who between them made hospital life quite different from the bleak and impersonal existence it can so easily be. It is impossible for a normal person to like being unwell, but if one must be, it would be difficult to find a better place for it than 29 British Commonwealth Hospital. And it was run, without noticeable friction, by British, Australian and Canadians. The patients were from all parts of the Commonwealth.

As in the Division itself, it is pleasant to see that some people, at least, whose homes are thousands of miles apart, can get on and work together in harmony. It is not as if we really spoke the same language. Have you ever tried to converse with a soldier of the "Van Doos" or Royal 22eme Regiment of Canada? Have you ever tried to persuade an Australian that it is not you who speak with an accent, but himself? It is better not to bother, but to take them as they come.

# NEWSLETTERS

This is the first of two newsletters collated by The Late Captain R.B Kettle; it was delayed for almost four months because the Chinese were unaware of our arrival. Volunteers from the Association Committee distributed them to relatives.
They are in their original format.

The object of these notes is to provide a background to the letters which individual members of the regiment send home. The daily round of military life varies little from continent to continent, and routine in Korea is not far removed from that in use when the regiment was operating in Europe or stationed in England.

For this reason, letters home in a static period of war make dull reading unless the reader can imagine the background against which they are written.

Prior to 1950, few British people had the misfortune to visit Korea, and naturally they must draw their information from the daily Press and other articles published in journals over the last two years. Popular journalism, to be attractive, must describe the sensational - the high spots and the low spots. The drab, ordinary, day-to-day details of life are very uninteresting to the average reader. For this reason, something further is required to fill the gaps, and in their modest way these notes hope to do so.

## The Country and People

When one speaks of one's knowledge of South Korea as a soldier, it is as well first to remember that this knowledge consists only of a 36-hour train journey from Pusan to the Army railhead at Uijongbu, a single trip to Seoul, the capital, and a fairly intimate knowledge of the geography of the Divisional area - an area some 15 miles from East to West, and 20 miles from North to South.

The Divisional area is divided neatly in half from East to West by the River Imjin, and the country on both sides of the river consists solely of mountain heights, valleys and streams converging in every variety of shape and contour on the main river basin. The valleys are completely flat and very narrow, few being wider than half a mile. These have a stream running down their centre, are planted with rice and are divided into fields by mud banks 18 inches high, which control the flow of the water. From the valley floor the hills rise steeply, culminating in rocks and boulders at an average height of 400 - 500 feet, with the two biggest peaks reaching 1200 - 2000 feet. Down every hill runs a series of water courses, which feed the streams after a rainstorm.

Millet, a form of wheat, is grown on the lowest slopes of the more gently sloping hills. Above that the slopes are wild and covered with stunted bushes, shrubs and evergreens.

Dotted about are small villages joined by mountain tracks. These will be described later.

The lack of roads is most striking to anyone unaccustomed to the Far East. Prior to the United Nations' arrival in the theatre, there was only one road in the Commonwealth sector, and this ran North-South and was crossed by two minor roads. Now a vast network of roads exists, these having all been bulldozed and maintained by American Army engineers. In this area alone, the engineer effort to construct and maintain 100 miles of road is immense.

When one lives in tents and bivouacs, a most important factor is the weather. Quite apart from changes in temperature, the outstanding feature of the last six months has been that the number of wet days has been under a dozen. This is indeed a boon, as wet clothes and no drying facilities are the bane of any camper. The months of December and January are dry and cold, with a fair wind blowing from the North (and incidentally Siberia) at intervals. The temperature runs in cycles of three to four days - three days sunny and thawing by day, followed by three days of hard frost.

# TRACKS IN KOREA

Snow fell heavily on several days, but disappeared rapidly from all except the hill tops, either by thawing or being blown away. Nightly frost readings showed 10 to 12 degrees of frost in early December, with increasing frost every night.

February was the coldest month and the lowest temperature was recorded during the night of Feb. 4th-5th, when 44 degrees of frost were registered. By the turn of the month and the beginning of March, however, it was obvious that the winter was over and, although nightly frosts occurred until April 28th, the day temperatures rose gradually and reached a peak of 55°F. during Easter week. Again the weather cycle repeated itself, and three warm days were usually followed by three of rain, wind or sleet.

After Easter a spell of blustery cold weather continued until the last week of April, when the wind dropped and temperatures soared into the eighties, where they have remained for the month of May.

But what of the local inhabitants? In the forward areas civilians have been evacuated and only Korean Service Corps labourers have been allowed to remain. The villages are burnt down to prevent their use by guerillas or Communist agents. South of the River Imjin the civilians were allowed to remain, and continued to cultivate their land. The houses are straw and mud huts of a single room, wherein the whole family and the cow lives. Signs of the Army's presence are the pickings from military rubbish dumps which litter every village. Beer bottles, packing cases, tins and scraps of clothing and boots make these groups of huts even more squalid. But if you go 40 miles South - away from the U.N. troops - you come upon cleaner villages where life has returned to normal and small bazaars exist to supply the needs of the villagers. It is a curious thought that roughly along the line of the 38th Parallel stands a modern Army of the United Nations barring the advance of the Communist forces. Yet 40 miles behind this force the Koreans live in exactly the same manner, one imagines, as their predecessors of 500 years ago. Their horizon appears to the foreign observer to be that of the next rice harvest and fuel for the coming winter. Communism, democracy and the United Nations would seem to be words as far above their heads as the clouds in the sky.

Individual craftsmen abound and their skill as hut makers, thatchers, carpenters and blacksmiths is being utilised by all.

Oriental in outlook, they vary from the white-skinned true Korean to the yellow skins of those who have Japanese blood. This country was for 200 years part of the Japanese Empire, and Seoul and Pusan are typical examples of the Japanese industrialisation and Western building.

The native religion is primitive and does not fall into any popular category. About 2 or 3 per cent are Christians.

### The Commonwealth Division

With that introduction to Korea, the notes pass on to a brief survey of the Division to which we belong and its place in the United Nations Forces.

Apart from the British Commonwealth Division, all other national units in Korea are integrated into American divisions. They wear U.S. uniform with appropriate national shoulder titles, use U.S. Army equipment and are administered by American Army services. The ROK (Republic of Korea) Divisions are similarly organised and equipped, but have a leavening of U.S. staff officers at all command levels.

The 1st Commonwealth Division is different; historically different is not too strong a word to use. Organised and equipped as a standard infantry division with an armoured regiment under command, its command, tactics and administration are no different from that practised in Germany and the Middle East, or taught in military schools in England.

# NEWSLETTERS

Its members are drawn from Great Britain, Canada, Australia, New Zealand and India.

The Divisional Staff is as mixed as the units. The General comes from England, his GSO I and ADC are Canadian, the AA & QMG English, and the Intelligence staff comes from Australia and New Zealand. The Divisional Commander is responsible to five independent Governments. What a chance for indecision, order and counter order! But in the past year this Division has won a place high in the praise of the United States Army Commander, and has shown a fitness for battle unsurpassed by any division in Korea.

At the lowest level the private soldiers have got to know each other and to joke and laugh over a pint of beer. A feature that has been particularly noticeable to Englishmen is the tremendous feeling of patriotism and allegiance to the British Crown shown by all these Dominion troops.

The Dominion contingents all vary in their composition, and it is interesting to compare them.

The British regiments and units are made up of Regular soldiers and National Servicemen in approximately equal numbers. The officers are largely Regular and, although the bulk of the British soldiers are very young, most senior ranks have considerable experience and service.

The Australians and New Zealanders, on the other hand, make up their forces differently. Both countries have very small permanent forces, usually in cadre form, and the greater majority of their men are recruited direct from civilian life on an 18 months' engagement to serve in Korea. They are extremely efficient, tough and hard-living. Their average age of other ranks is probably higher than ours, but in contrast their officers are very much younger. Battalion Commanders in their thirties and Company Commanders in their early twenties give an idea of their age structure.

The Canadians produce a compromise between the British and Australian systems. Although possessing only a small permanent force, it is expanding rapidly, as can be seen by the arrival of the 27th Canadian Infantry Brigade in Germany. Most Canadian officers and a small proportion of other ranks are now Regulars. The balance is made up of ex-Servicemen of the 1939-45 War specially enlisted for 18 months in Korea. As a result they tend to be rather older than our own men.

The Indian contingent is an airborne field ambulance unit. Every man is a Regular and a parachutist. They are the only airborne medical unit in Korea and have a high reputation. They are extremely smart, and their maroon berets give them a fine distinguishing mark.

## The Task of the Regiment

The Regiment landed at Pusan from HMT "Georgic" on 2 Dec 51, just after the truce negotiators had agreed on a cease-fire line which would be acceptable to both sides in the event of the remaining armistice terms being agreed upon. A 30-day time limit was given to clear the outstanding clauses, but this period passed with little progress being made. However, the United Nations considered that, their military objective having been obtained, further offensive action by them on the ground would achieve nothing towards peace and would only cause unnecessary casualties.

The result has been that since we landed there has been no change in positions. This, however, did not mean in any way an unofficial cease-fire, as these notes will show.

# TRACKS IN KOREA

### Mail and Welfare Gifts

This subject has been purposely left to the last to emphasise its value and to show how much we appreciate the mail. Airmail arrives at Seoul airport by Australian Transport Command aircraft, and from there it goes by truck to the Divisional Post Office - a distance of some 30 miles. It is already sorted into unit sacks and is collected by the Regimental Post Corporal, who sorts it into squadron bundles. This takes any time up to an hour so that, by the time it is ready, the squadron representatives are standing by to drive it up to the squadron areas for distribution to individuals. Mail days are Tuesday, Thursday and Saturday, and these form the highlights of the week.

Sea mail and welfare parcels take considerably longer, averaging 6 weeks to 2 months from the time of posting in England. There is usually one delivery a month, but this depends entirely on the arrivals of ships at Kure, in Japan.

You will be glad to know that we have been plentifully supplied with additional warm clothing, dart boards, cards, pipes and every kind of indoor game by the Regimental Association and numerous WVS centres. The latter have been particularly good at supplying magazines, periodicals and books, which are very much appreciated.

It is very obvious that a lot of hard work and ingenuity has gone into the continuous preparation and despatching of these gifts, and we would like people at home to realise how much their work is appreciated.

Mail cannot come too often, and we would ask you to keep on writing to your sons and husbands - even the most trivial home news is wanted.

As is probably generally known, the Regiment is to be relieved by the 1st Royal Tank Regiment in the winter and expects to be stationed in the Middle East for the next two years.

Whatever one's present views on Korea may be, when one year out here is over it will certainly be an experience to look back on, and no doubt will be the background for many a good story in the future.

R.B.K.

## Editorial

It is now 60 years since Rupert Kettle wrote this letter. Little did he know that North and South Korea would still be a divided nation. The letter further demonstrates the good fortune I feel to be in a position to report it to a vastly changed world. Rupert himself died in a road accident in 1980.

## Ex Sergeant "Derek" Wetmore sent in his memories from Australia.

He served as Regimental Signal Sergeant throughout our tour.

"Prior to departure for Korea I had been instructing at the RAC depot in Bovington. I rejoined in Aldershot and immediately updated our commanders and operators who would have to use the UN phonetic alphabet and procedures which was being used by the Americans. Alpha, Baker, Charlie, Dog became Alpha, Bravo, Charlie, Delta. It was not intended that I should go to Korea but persuasion from characters like Partridge, Voisey, Peacock, Alan Claydon and others caused me to volunteer. Korea gave me an opportunity as Signals Sergeant to put into practice what I had been teaching at Bovington during a four year tour of duty.

During the cold spells of -40 degrees tanks had to be started at two hourly intervals to prevent frozen cylinder blocks and to keep batteries operational over a 24 hour period. I remember that bread, eggs and beer froze solid too. Only a week after arrival there was a tragic event causing the death of Signalman Lathem who had joined us as part of a Royal Signals detachment which from 1938 until 1965 was assigned to us for the purpose of repairing radios.

A tank was taken to the top of a hill for better reception as a relay station. Its brakes failed and it rolled backwards and flattened two bivouacs where Latham and Craftsman Cummins were sleeping. Cummins suffered serious injuries, Latham was killed. There was also the complete destruction of a Bedford truck given the title of "Hell Hole", which was the Regimental Command Post as a result of an oil stove being knocked over. That resulted in the construction of Hell Hole 2 by excavating a bunker into the side of a hill and heavily fortifying it with sandbags, we included two 19 sets and a ten line S.U.V telephone exchange. This had to be manned for twenty-four hours daily and was staffed by our own operators and Royal Signals personal. They formed a very efficient service and included National Servicemen. There was a panic when a large snake had made its abode in the wall.

During Operation JEHU and while I was operating on the Commanding Officers tank, "HUMERIST", I had been excluded from the briefings. The Regimental Signals Officer had attended but for some unknown reason was not on the operation. It all sounded very chaotic. The CO was trying to ascertain which tanks were bogged down and those out of action from mines. I only made sense of it when I read the write up in the reports in "Change and Challenge," some years later.

When necessary I had to be on loan to the squadrons to relieve a crew commander on R&R or sick. While attached to Lieutenant Taylor's troop supporting the Welsh Regiment, the crew drew my attention to a mechanical problem requiring me to dismount and inspect one of the driving sprockets. It coincided with the early morning netting call involving 72 out stations. For the Regimental Signals Sergeant to miss this was unforgivable. It was a ritual! I was the only station not to answer. As a punishment I was ordered to stay on the set for the rest of the day. I always felt that I had been set-up! On another occasion I was sent to our HAD (Heavy Aid Detachment) REME to modify an armoured Half Track vehicle into a Communication Vehicle which was to house three 19 sets and a ten line telephone exchange, plus a cable-layer (a cylindrical drum which rotated to lay a cable along a track-side). Whilst watching the welding operation too closely, I developed "welders glare". Heavily tinted glasses should have been worn. As a result I was hospitalised. I thought I was permanently blind. Eye drops were the cure. I was discharged but still without perfect sight and this contributed to an accident with burns to my left arm and face. The whole incident made me deeply aware of the complexity and effectiveness of the UN organisation. I never found out who put the flames out, who covered my arms with anti-burns ointment or who organised the medical half-track to take me to the Indian MASH (medical aid and surgical hospital). I was then transferred to NORMASH (the Norwegian field hospital) in a Dodge ambulance with a Korean driver. I was put into a bed next to a GI who had just died from drinking Korean hooch, probably Sake, a potent rice drink. After treatment I was moved to a Canadian dressing unit in Seoul. The whole treatment left me with the happy memory of excellent treatment and wonderful food during the recovery. After two weeks I was delivered to a British convalescent centre in Inchon, run by WVS ladies who were absolutely superb. It was here that I formed a friendship with some French Canadians, a rough lot but it was a hilarious stay. Finally it was back to Tactical Headquarters. I realised that I had rubbed shoulders with Indians, Koreans, Canadians, Norwegians, Americans and our own Brits. A truly international event.

Now aged 82 I still serve with the local Fire Brigade as Communications Officer. There is a Radio Schedule at 09.30 hours every Sunday. I have never missed a call, my friends never know why."

# A NAVAL VENTURE
## Major General Henry Woods recounts

It was a bright sunny morning in the early summer as the two Auster light aircraft lifted off the grassy runway of the Divisional Flight just south of the Pintail Bridge over the River Imjin. I and my clobber were passengers in one, David Rowat similarly in the other. We had responded to an offer of two days afloat with the Royal Navy Task Force in the open sea beyond the estuary of the River Han. A kind friend, the Flight Commander, offered to fly us south to the air base just south of Seoul. We accepted gratefully.

The great bulk of Kamak-san disappeared beneath us and all too soon we deplaned, thanked the pilots and reported to the Flight Centre for a Dakota flight out to one of the island bases. Here arose snag No.1. The plane was already full with higher priority passengers, there were no further flights for 48 hours, and our adventure seemed over before it had begun. I spied a group of US Army light aircraft and found they were tasked by the Chief of Staff to the Commander 8th US Army. He was a friend from a spell at the Armour School, Fort Knox, Kentucky two years before, and, after I had explained our problem, we were soon bundled into two aircraft and climbing through the permanent smoky haze which hid the city from us. Snag No.2 was that no one had said in all the planning where the island base was, for reasons of security. All too soon the pilots, now at the limit of their range, landed on a little strip at one end of which a burnt out fighter stood on its nose. A Jeep whose aerial mast swung to and fro was lurching along the track to the strip and we were greeted by a US Captain who explained that he ran a guerrilla outfit raiding the North Korean mainland only a very few miles from "his" island. We shouted our thanks to the American pilots,

# A NAVAL VENTURE

who headed for home, and were taken to the "guerrillas'" HQ, a low ceilinged Korean house in a clump of trees.

Snag No.3 was that his radio, powered by a bicycle generator manned by a succession of Korean cyclists, was not in touch with the Royal Navy. Throughout the afternoon all our efforts seemed to fail, I was wondering how we were going to return to Seoul. David remained calm and unruffled in what must have seemed to him a madcap enterprise. We sat and dozed, made further attempts to pass a message to the Navy and had a curious rice dish of food. Sometime after dark, we were told that a Korean gunboat would pick us up and take us to one of HM ships. Around midnight we stumbled along a narrow path to the shore and embarked in a seriously overloaded rubber dinghy with a sputtering outboard engine. Slowly against the fierce rip tide of the Han River the dingy closed with the gunboat, which we boarded with relief and damp backsides.

We were shown into a minute Wardroom, The Captain smiled and bowed but neither he nor any of the crew knew any language other than Korean. We dozed with our heads on the wardroom table, until we realised that the sky had paled and dawn was breaking. Fine on the bow was the island's base and steaming away from us towards the open sea were the ships of the RN Task Force led by the cruiser, HMS Newcastle. The Korean gunboat came alongside the destroyer Cossack which took us on board. Snag No.4 was an extremely angry destroyer Captain who did not mince his nautical vocabulary. Our thoughtlessness in getting ourselves onto another island, and causing the Korean motor gunboat to quit its station in rescuing us imperilled operations. We tried to look penitent and hang dog and I mumbled an apology. We were dismissed to the Wardroom, given a hearty breakfast, the opportunity to wash and shave and a tour of the ship. Our hosts could not have been kinder, once the Captain had quietened down and the spirit of the ship's company was the same as in the Regiment.

Late in the afternoon we went ashore and joined the passengers on the Dakota flight back to Seoul, followed by a bumpy ride in a Jeep up the main axis, whose surface was corrugated by American six wheelers. We regaled our brother officers with our account of the Korean navy lark, or how not to endear oneself to the Royal Navy! Whether they believed us I do not know, but the tale is all true.

# "AN EARLY FLIGHT"
by the editor

An attempt to become a pilot in the Army Air Corps was a failure in endeavour but had a very advantageous knock on effect.

During a visit to Regimental Headquarters I met a Sergeant pilot, "Red" Meeton who was an Auster pilot based at Fort George Rear. I had told him of my thwarted attempt to be a parachutist and later a Glider Pilot. He informed me that the Air Corps was appealing for pilots and highly recommended it. I arranged to meet our Commanding Officer, Lieut Colonel Arthur Carr. The interview lasted less than five minutes. "Do you realise that the upper age limit is twenty-three?" he asked. "Yes", I replied but I am informed that some exceptions are considered and it could be after our year in Korea. "You are twenty-six and do not qualify", he replied, "and you will not be going. Full stop." I called at the Airfield on my way back and informed "Red". This resulted in an early call on the land line instructing me to be at Fort George at 07.30 hours to act as observer on a routine morning flight. It was a wonderful break in the daily routine and was to be very beneficial twelve years later.

The pilot, Captain Peter Wilson explained that we would climb to 7,500 feet over our own lines and then patrol the eight mile front keeping a watch on any movement and particularly puffs of smoke from a mortar or field gun. I was given a map and fitted with a Reserve Parachute which is smaller than a main 'chute and used as a seat. My head was already touching the fuselage above me. What a pleasure to see the other side of the front. On the Commonwealth side the roads were busy; there were towels and mess tins hanging on bushes and plenty of other evidence of occupation. On the Chinese side there was no movement at all. A long, wide trench was pointed out and used mainly at night for supplies. With the doors removed it was quite cold but bearable. The patrol passed without incident. Peter Wilson informed me that there was a large bundle of books he wished to deliver to a friend who was located in a trench on the top of a hill. A rapid decent to the rear and fast approach up the slope and a shout to me and the bundle had gone. A quick bank and back over the hill and return to base. I had a repeat performance about a month later. It strengthened my resolve to in some way to achieve my childhood dream to be a pilot. I now had a contact with "Red Meeton" and his Flight Commander, Captain Peter Downwood, who was later to become a Major General and become Commandant of the Royal Hospital, Chelsea. Both were helpful in later life. In 1963 when about to retire, my Commanding Officer, Gavin Murray, asked me what I intended to do. He was well aware of my flying ambitions. I had been offered a Quartermasters Commission but had declined it. I informed Colonel Gavin that I had decided to do something different but had no idea what. "Pity", he replied, "the Army Air Corps are offering you an appointment as Adjutant to 651 Flight AAC which is about to be deployed to Cyprus in the rank of Captain." From this I had a most enjoyable seven year extension and as much flying as I wanted. "Red" Meeton was a major commanding one of the Flights, Peter Wilson was a Staff Officer in MP6, the branch responsible for the AAC manning. It proved to be the happiest ending to my service care.

# AN EARLY FLIGHT

14th Field Regiment, Royal Artillery positions in the Commonwealth area, summer 1952. (Imperial Wa Museum).

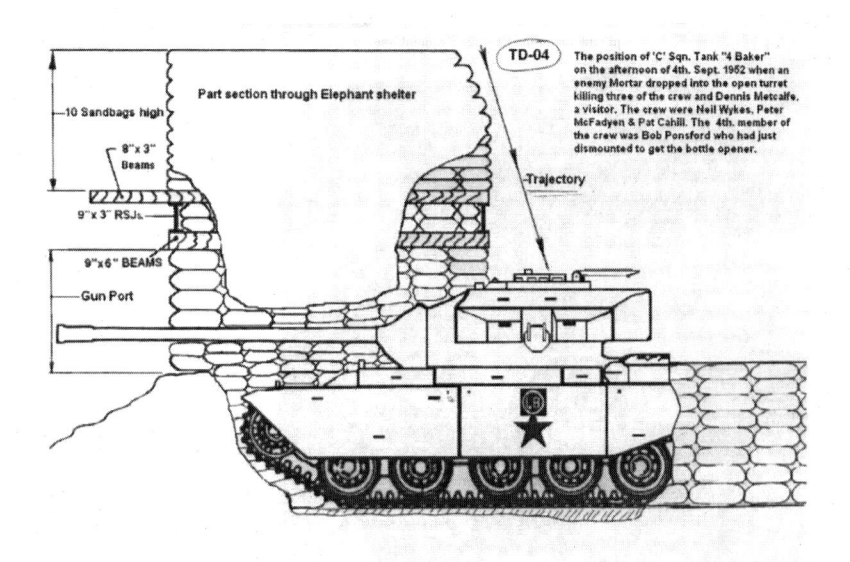

Part section through Elephant shelter

-10 Sandbags high
8"x 3" Beams
9"x 3" RSJs
9"x 6" BEAMS
Gun Port

TD-04  The position of 'C' Sqn. Tank "4 Baker" on the afternoon of 4th. Sept. 1952 when an enemy Mortar dropped into the open turret killing three of the crew and Dennis Metcalfe, a visitor. The crew were Neil Wykes, Peter McFadyen & Pat Cahill. The 4th. member of the crew was Bob Ponsford who had just dismounted to get the bottle opener.

Trajectory

143

TRACKS IN KOREA

GLW-049  Rear view of experimental RE built 'Elephant Shelter' with 'C' Sqn. 4 Troop tank '4 Baker' in position. Bob Ponsford, Arthur Baxter & Paddy Cahill atop. Baxter had just delivered the mail. Later that same day a mortar dropped into the open cupola killing Paddy Cahill, Jock McFadyen, Neil Vykes and Dennis Metcalfe.

Bunker built by the Royal Engineers to protect the Centurion tank of 5DG on Point 187, August 1952.
(5th Royal Inniskilling Dragoon Guards)

AN EARLY FLIGHT

Tank entering the bunker.
(5th Royal Inniskilling Dragoon Guards).

Paul LeMercier, 'Poggy' Cooper on tank '2Baker' 'A'Sqn.
with front of tank under Elephant shelter.

## The regimental history, 'Change and Challenge' records

In place of the winter's steady trickle of space-heater fires in tents and bunkers, with the attendant disciplinary action over burnt clothing and equipment, the Korean summer now upon us meant issues of Paludrine and salt tablets, bathing in the River Imjin and a careful watch for snakes and rats. Some succumbed to a local virus infection called 'Songo' fever, which involved a days' rest in the Norwegian Mobile Army Surgical Hospital, looked after by their popular nurses. The Divisional Air OP flight were diverted to spraying marshy areas where mosquitoes might breed, and parties from the regiment went on five days R and R (Rest and Recuperation) Leave to Japan. Major Walker brought back a loo seat for the rough-hewn Officers' 'thunderbox'. A few spent two or three days afloat with ships of the Royal Navy, and some Officers, after attending short courses as forward air controllers, were soon up in the slow propeller-driven Harvards which circled over the forward areas and guided the jet ground-attack aircraft onto their targets.

When the monsoon season began in late June, issues of extra tents, flood precautions and many ingenious improvisations had made the reserve squadron camps very comfortable. The River Imjin was due to become a raging torrent threatening the supply routes over the Bailey Bridges across it, and 'B' Squadron practised shooting at debris which might damage the piers. Before the monsoon broke on 29 June, reducing both visibility and warlike activities, 'A' Squadron had supported a raid on Point 227 by B Company Welsh Regiment, Corporal Steggles was fatally wounded in a machine-gun accident, and Lieutenant Rowat (3rd Troop 'C' Squadron) was slightly wounded by enemy mortar fire. Sergeant Irving assumed command of 3rd Troop on Point 159, and his tank was hit 30 times by field artillery shells, being replaced twice in a fortnight owing to the damage sustained. He was awarded the MM (Military Medal) for his fearless but cheerful leadership and determination. Thus the enemy strove for nearly three weeks in July to drive our tanks off the crest.

These rains caused the Imjin River to spate, and forced the closure of the Pintail Bridge between Divisional HQ and Regimental HQ. Whilst the river normally flowed quietly through a gorge 130 feet below the Pintail roadway, the swirling swift torrent was now only a few feet from the roadway, and whole trees were swept along. The level did not fall or the bridge re-open until 31 July, and the Echelon trucks were soon busy replenishing the depleted stocks held forward of the river. Twice more in August the rains came down, the river spated and this time troops of 'A' Squadron as well as 'B' practised their gunnery skills on the large debris above the Pintail bridge and, further downstream, the Teal crossing, on the route back to Gloucester Valley.

Both August and September were principally marked by spasmodic enemy artillery 'hates' on forward tank positions. Despite the newly built overhead protection over 4B on Point 187, on 5 September by a million-to-one chance, an HE shell entered the turret and killed the crew (Sergeant Wykes, Lance Corporal Metcalfe, Troopers' Cahill and McFadyen). By the end of September the heavy rains had ceased, the humidity declined, and the pace of life quickened. 'A' Squadron, in reserve, trained actively with newly arrived infantry battalions like the 1st King's Regiment, and the new Divisional Commander, Major-General Michael West, visited RHQ and 'A' Squadron.

Dummy tanks were introduced onto a prominent feature which had been temporarily occupied by 2nd Troop 'A' Squadron for 24 hours. Each day radio communications were checked at frequent intervals and the regimental command net, like the Windmill Theatre, could boast that it never closed. Every month the American-style call signs were changed and those who had been 'Betty Boop' became 'Symbolic' and then 'Congenial'. The scope for humorous alterations (shambolic and congenial) may be imagined, but from doggerel verse published in the Journal the following stanza gives the best flavour of 1st Troop 'B' on the air:

> Frankenstein One, Frankenstein One
> They talk so much that nothing gets done
> Barnes, McCallum, Cowling, McGinn,
> Believe in discussion before they begin
> Astounding manoeuvres down slippery banks
> To prove the existence of somersault tanks".

The mountains and hills were tinted by vivid autumn colours, the nights were much cooler, and the regiment went back into the ubiquitous Jerseys Wool Heavy. For the first time in the regiment those worn by Officers and senior ranks were green, having been dyed in Japan. A flock of wild geese in flight became a radar sighting of enemy aircraft which caused a 'flash red' alert soon after lunch on 5th October, while an attempt the next day to control indirect fire from tank guns by an OP airborne in an Auster light aircraft was a failure, the fall of shot not being observed.

The Squadrons were soon accustomed to the operational routine of a month in the forward areas followed by a month in reserve. During the first six months, despite the snail's pace of the truce talks at Panmunjom, the enemy's activities belied any prospects of peace. The Chinese brought up more mortars, guns and ammunition, and the scale and weight of enemy artillery fire perceptibly increased. In some areas the enemy inched his defensive positions closer to our own forward defended localities, while his patrols were more active throughout no- man's land. The Squadrons played their part in British counter measures by sending troop leaders out with our infantry patrols and by improving the reaction time and accuracy of tank fire support, registering targets during the day and laying the tank guns on fixed lines with switches recorded by night. A patrol in trouble only had to give a code word by radio, and very effective fire was brought down speedily by the tanks as well as the artillery and mortars.

******

Point 227, once tree covered, had become a desolate sandy shell-torn waste whose crest lay in no man's land after the British had failed to hold it the previous November because it enfiladed Chinese positions to the west and south. It was a most sensitive area for both sides. On 25 January, 'A' Squadron, less one troop, provided close fire support to a raid on this feature by two platoons 3rd Battalion Royal Australian Regiment. The value of the tank fire was particularly evident during the tricky withdrawal, as the enemy reacted very vigorously with drenching mortar and artillery fire and a counterattack.

Declining numbers, as National Servicemen departed for home, forced the regiment to reduce overheads by moving A Echelon to RHQ. Nevertheless RHQ Tank Troop continued to try to drown ribald comments about their 'cushy' lifestyle by regular spells in the line, and in October they were with 'B'. In anticipation of our relief by 1st Royal Tank Regiment at the end of the year, six of the Troop Leaders were attached to the Regiment in September and early in November their advance party would replace ours as it departed for the Canal Zone in Egypt, our new station in 1953.

The Balaclava anniversary was celebrated appropriately on 25th October with a church parade and service in 'C' Squadron's camp, at which the Band of the 3rd Royal Australian Regiment played. After lunch the pipes and drums of the Black Watch performed amid 'C' Squadron's fun fair and mingled with inter-squadron football and tug-of-war.

In early November the Black Watch with 4th Troop 'B' had relieved the American Marines on the vital ridge features west of the Samichon River nicknamed 'Hook', 'Warsaw' and 'Ronson'. From mid-November sharply increased shelling, mortaring and enemy patrol activity forewarned us of intense enemy activity forward of the 'Hook' and an attack on the Black Watch company very well dug in on its reverse slope. At 21.00, on 18th November very heavy artillery fire and large-scale enemy movement beyond our wire signalled the start of a vicious Chinese attack. Trooper Brindley remembers: "4th Troop was sitting it out with the Black Watch just behind the skyline in a dugout with a wireless extension from Centurion 4C, and soon realised they were for it. Running the few yards to our tank we survived many mortar shells bursting amongst us, and we were soon on the move, myself driving with headlights on, and still uncertain if small arms fire directed at them was from our lads or the Chinese. We received many direct hits ('Tokios'), just like being in a bell".

'Ronson'

# THE HOOK

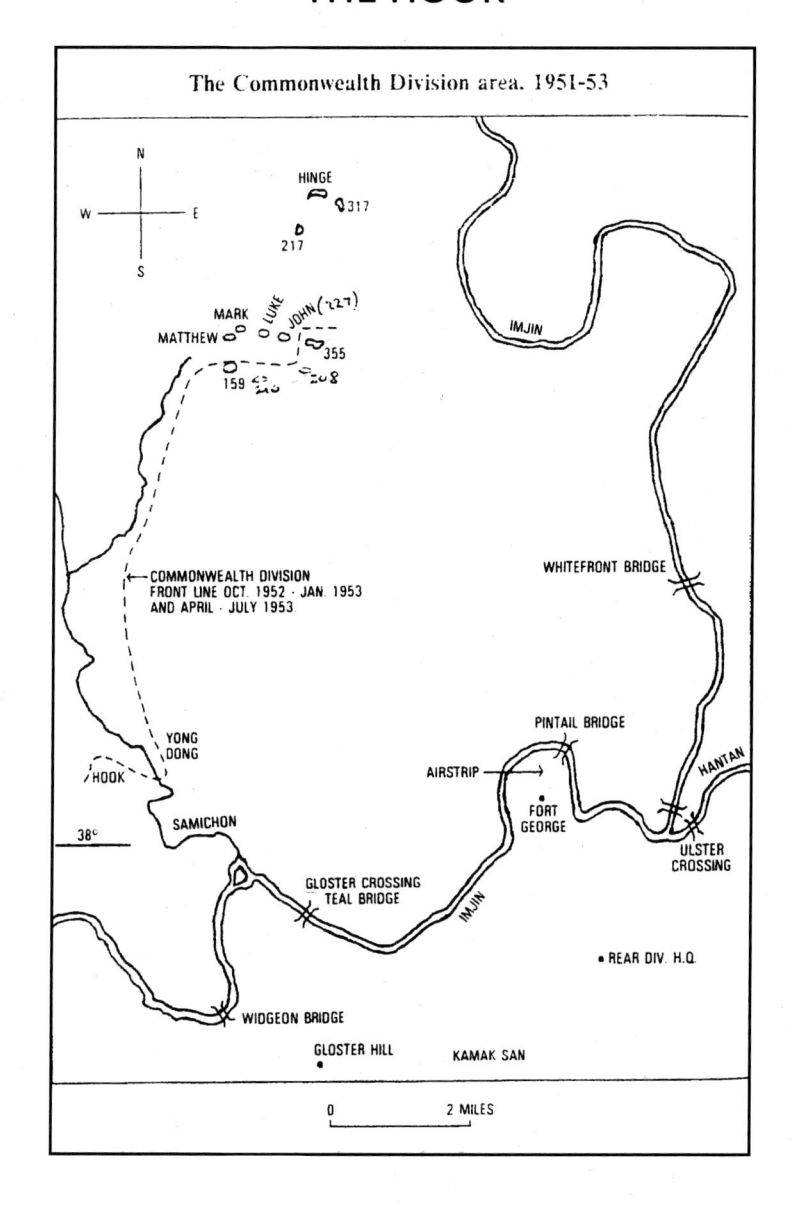

# TRACKS IN KOREA

4th Troop
*Lieutenant MJC Anstice*
(Michael Anstice was awarded an immediate Military Cross).

The Troop deployed in two halves at either end of the ridge-line and, assisted by the fifth tank firing from east of the river, joined our own artillery, mortars and machine-guns in bringing down heavy fire on the enemy's forming up areas and axes of advance. American tank searchlights had been fitted to our tanks and were effective in illuminating targets until the smoke of battle grew dense or the enemy fire damaged them. The Chinese attack overran the forward platoon of A Company 1st Black Watch, who however withdrew into their bunkers, gallantly called down artillery defensive fire onto their own position, and emerged at 2225 to drive the last of the enemy off their position.

Prefaced by activity in no man's land, at 00.37 a fresh Chinese attack was made from the direction of 'Warsaw'. Lieutenant Anstice reported that.

"The 'Hook' was the name given by the American Army to a small group of hills forming the shape of a hook and dominating the main route to Seoul (capital of South Korea) when approached from the north. More lives were lost on this insignificant, but vital feature than anywhere else during the three years of the Korean War. By the end of 1951 the fluid period of the Korean War had come to a halt on what came to be known as the 38th parallel, and the two armies, United Nations and Chinese (Peoples Liberation Army) faced each other over paddy fields. Distance between the two sides in many places could be measured in yards, and the style of soldiering very similar to the 1914-18 War. Both sides were establishing ever improving trench systems, and fighting was limited to the occasional company raid, frequent and deadly shell or mortar fire. Minefields occupied much of no-man's land.

The Commonwealth Division, of which we were the armoured

# THE HOOK

support regiment, occupied the front line to the North East of Seoul. At any one time, two Sqns would be forward and the remaining one in reserve south of the River Imjin. Each Infantry Battalion, Australian, Canadian or British had in close support 1 Troop of 4 Centurion tanks of ours. Crossing the River Imjin meant using two American built bridges named Teal and Widgeon, although in the summer, tanks could, and did, ford the river with ease. On the Chinese side the aforementioned 'Hook', dominated the Samichon Valley which made up no-man's land and the Imjin River crossings behind the allied lines. The feature was occupied by the allied forces having been seized from the Chinese at great cost. Since the Hook was from the Chinese point of view an essential part of their defences it is hardly surprising that they wished to recapture it regardless of loss of life.

In Oct 1952, 4th Troop, B Squadron (my Troop) in support of the 1st Battalion The Black Watch occupied a position on the left flank of the Commonwealth Division at a point on the front line called Yong Dong. To our front across the Samichon Valley was the 'Hook', which was then occupied by two Companies of the 7th US Marines. The 7th consisted of 3 Bns tasked with defending on a 6 miles front with only one company in reserve. To use a well-known British adage, there was no 'defence in depth'. It was not long after our arrival at Yong Dong that we were told that the Commonwealth Division was to reposition to the west and relieve the US Marines. Colonel Rose, CO. The Black Watch, crossed to the Hook to see the situation for himself. He found a supremely over confident unit of Marines, one of whom showed him his 'Hootchie' from which he demonstrated how he could pot the advancing Chinese from his sandbagged window while still on his bed. No real attempt had been made to construct a position as impregnable as possible. The Hook was woefully undermanned.

It is necessary at this stage to describe the Hook feature. A deep salient pointing north, it was protected by two outposts: Warsaw, 600 yards to the North East and Ronson 275 yards west which replaced the already enemy-seized Seattle. Opposite the marines were two Chinese

Regts and 120 pieces of artillery. For many months the Chinese had been digging an intricate system of trenches getting ever closer to the American outposts and from which they intended to launch their attack. It could be said that the Chinese already shared the northern part of the Hook.

On 24th Oct, the Chinese barrage began directed against the Hook, Ronson and Warsaw. About 2,850 Artillery and Mortar rounds devastated bunkers, trenches and communication lines. The destruction exceeded the Marines ability to repair the damage, and the forthcoming attack was well advertised. At 6.10pm, 26th Oct, the 3rd Battalion, 357th Regt attacked. Ronson was overrun – nobody survived. By 7pm there was hand-to-hand fighting on Warsaw and Artillery and Mortar fire smothered the Hook. By 11.30pm Warsaw had fallen and the enemy had started overrunning the main defence system. As morning broke we could see through our turret mounted peri-binoculars the Chinese infantry slowly progressing down the trenches on the Hook and its neighbouring defence position. We were

# THE HOOK

tuned into the American net and heard one after another messages cut short at the same time as we observed the Chinese arrival at each section command post. By the end of the day the Chinese were in control of the whole area in spite of several attempted counterattacks and support from the air using napalm and high explosive. We were supporting, as best we could, firing across the valley, but to little effect. We had a birds' eye view of the unfolding tragedy – a memory forever etched on my mind. In the afternoon of the 27th, the US 1st Marines, brought in to help the hard pressed 7$^{th}$ who started the counterattack. It was not until 6am on the 28th that the Marines finally retook the Hook and finally secured Ronson and Warsaw. This was the first battle of the Hook: 70 Marines were killed, 386 wounded and 39 missing. The Chinese were thought to have fired in the region of 15,500 rounds of artillery and mortar, not to mention allied artillery and air strikes. Two Medals of Honour were awarded to members of the US forces.

It was now our turn. As planned, The Black Watch supported by 4th Troop moved across the Samichon at night and at daylight found ourselves faced with a wasteland. Everything was pulverised and trenches collapsed. We knew that another attack was imminent and little time was available to reconstruct the defences. Colonel Rose had witnessed the fate of the Americans and decided that an entirely different defensive strategy was necessary: His plan was to reconstruct the original trench system which effectively circled the main Hook feature. At suitable points, L shaped tunnels were to be dug from the trenches into the side of the hill, each tunnel to accommodate a section of infantry. 'A' Company, under the Command of Major Angus Irwin, was allotted the task of defending the Hook. Work started immediately. Sappers and Jocks worked day and night constructing shell proof bunkers on Ronson and Warsaw and the Hook. Much of the work was carried out under the noses of the enemy. The well-known picture of the Hook depicts the project progressing lit by star shells and flares. Standing patrols were established each night on Ronson and Warsaw and withdrawn at daylight. We of 4th Troop worked equally hard to establish reserve ammunition bays and shell proof accommodation. Our four tanks were positioned with two close to the bottom of the Hook hill and two a short distance to the West with C Company between us. Our task was to enfilade the attacking Chinese infantry as they moved onto Ronson and the Hook. For this purpose we were fitted with searchlights mounted on the gun barrels. In those days, of course, there was no such thing as an infra-red night vision aid. While all this heavy work was going on the Chinese kept up their shell fire and Black Watch soldiers continued to be killed. Every morning I visited the front trenches of the Hook to check progress, each time brushing past a Chinese foot in basketball boot projecting from the trench wall.

Colonel Rose's plan was to fight off the attacking Chinese up to the last moment, order the Jocks to retreat into their tunnels and then bring down the whole of the Division Artillery onto the Chinese exposed in the open. At the appropriate moment in the battle it was planned that one of our tanks would climb a precipitous footpath/jeep track to the top of the Hook and, on turning North, lead the counterattack along the ridge. There was doubt as to whether a Centurion tank would manage such a task on such a narrow track cut into the side of the hill. We tried in daylight, lost a track, and retired having replaced the track under shell fire. Exercise over – or so we thought.

On the evening of the 18 Nov 1952, I was sitting on the turret of my tank 'standing to' enjoying a can of self-heating Oxtail soup when the ground erupted all round me. I remember saying, "this is it", jumped into the tank closing down as I did so. The Chinese barrage was intense and largely directed at us. They feared the Centurion with good reason. We started firing on fixed lines with our secondary armament (7.62 BESA co-axial mounted machine gun) using the lights of our searchlights. These lights proved useless as they reflected off the smoke from our own guns. It was only a short time anyway before they were destroyed by enemy shellfire as we were hit many times by the Chinese artillery. Due to being closed down the fumes in the turret were excessive and the auxiliary generator extraction fan could not cope with the gas generated by both the main armament and machine gun. I was violently ill and my loader/operator rendered unconscious. I sent for a replacement, and Corporal Williamson was brought out by Jeep from Sqn HQ. By this time the Chinese had overrun Ronson and Warsaw and were arriving on the Hook. The Black Watch had retreated into their tunnels and the Division Artillery decimated the Chinese caught out in the open. They were driven off taking their dead with them. There then ensued a brief lull until the fun started up again. Once again the Chinese attacked from Warsaw and Ronson. There were no longer outposts to hold up the attack, and the enemy were once again on the Hook. It was at this stage in the battle that Colonel Rose asked for a tank to lead the counterattack. I had already tried and failed to get up the Hook in the daylight rehearsal described earlier in this account. Tanks are highly vulnerable at night and are normally withdrawn from the battlefield for ammunition and fuel replacement. They form close leaguers for self-protection and sally forth at dawn. They do not drive blind into enemy infantry. I objected to the order on the grounds that we probably would fail to reach the objective and would likely be destroyed by infantry. My objection was overruled. It was I who had attempted to reach the top and failed, so it was I who had to try again, but in the dark this time.

At about 1am, I set off having first handed command of the Troop to Sergeant Nunn, my Troop Sergeant. We soon reached the bottom of the path and started to climb. Approximately half way up, my driver, Trooper Lewis, said on the intercom that our way was blocked. Indeed it was by a 15cwt truck and a jeep both belonging to the Gunner OP. I wirelessed for instructions, and was told to drive over them. This we did. The tank felt as though it was trying to climb a wall, and then subsided as it crushed the two vehicles completely flat. We continued up the path and reached the top, turning left at the company command post. We started to move forward firing our machine gun along the ridge when there was the most almighty flash and a thump heard through my headphones and a call from Taffy Lewis, my driver, that he had been hit. We could not see forward as the main armament cowling had caught fire and to add to our difficulties we were being subjected to heavy machine gun fire. Corporal Williamson gallantly leapt out and extinguished the fire which was not serious. The scene on the Hook was like Dante's inferno. Chinese Infantry again caught in the open and being subjected not only to our shells bursting before impact, but theirs too. We were stuck in the middle of this, immobile, and wondering what to do next.

The Chinese had witnessed our failed attempt to get a tank up the hill and rightly deduced that we would try again, so sent an ambush party with a 3.5 rocket launcher to intercept us. We were hit at point blank range and holed through the glacier plate. Fortunately the rocket failed to burn through the last fraction of an inch and on bursting blew the remaining metal into Trooper Lewis. We pulled Lewis through the driver's hatch into the turret where he lay on the floor, his body preventing the turret traversing. Corporal Williamson scrambled into the driver's compartment and with me directing and him driving, we reversed until there was room to turn and made our way back down the track, finishing off the jeep and truck en route.

Mortar fire was still heavy as we stopped outside The Black Watch regimental aid post which was conveniently on the way back to our original action station. Trooper Lewis was a big man lying inert on the turret floor. I have never forgotten the effort it took for Williamson, Trooper Marks (Gunner) and I to lift him up through the turret hatch and off the tank onto a stretcher. Williamson and I carried Lewis into the aid post. A loaded military stretcher is normally a four man job. We dropped Lewis twice as we tried to run through the mortar fire. The inside of the aid post is an everlasting memory. The yellow light of the hurricane lamps lit shadowy figures moving round inert bodies, some covered by blankets. The noise of exploding shells outside.

We returned to our original position and continued the battle from our hull down position. A relief driver was sent out from Sqn HQ. By

# THE HOOK

6am, all enemy were off the Hook. A Battalion of Princess Patricia's Light Infantry took over temporarily from The Black Watch. At about 8am, I received a message saying that the Chinese were about to attack again. All 4 tanks had withdrawn from their fire positions to replenish ammunition etc. I called up my Troop Sergeant to order him back to his fire position. The threatened attack never materialised. The extremely brave Chinese ambush party was found dead the following morning.

Due to Colonel Rose's outstanding leadership and tactical planning, The Black Watch, who had repelled a battalion attack on a company front, lost 16 killed, 82 wounded and 16 missing. During the battle, 16,000 rounds of 25pdr were fired. 4th Troop fired 150 rounds of 20pdr HE, 2200 of 105, 200 of 155 and 3200 rounds of 4.2 mortar. Three ripples each of 144 rockets were also directed onto the Hook.

No wonder I thought I was back again during my first experience of the Edinburgh fireworks".

The Samich'on river, summer, 1952
(Major J A Foulis, RAPC).

The remains of the Royal Artillery Willys Jeep and 15cwt truck after being crushed by a Centurion Mk.3 of Lt. M. Anstice, 4 Troop 'B' Sqn. 5th Royal Inniskilling Dragoon Guards, during the second battle of the Hook, 18th November 1952 (5RIDG)

Tpr. Wells, the gunner of 'Black Bob', holds aloft a 3.5in. bazooka rocket found on the day after the Hook battle in which the tank was pierced by bazooka, wounding the driver. The penetration hole can be seen in the glacis plate just below the driver's hatch beside Tpr. Wells. The hole was repaired by inserting a track pin, cut to length and then welded into position. (Peter Williamson).

Hook Trench System.

# REST AND RECOUPERATION....R&R

*Editorial*

During the year each of us was granted a few days leave in Tokyo, Japan, only an hour's flying time away. The period varied due to weather which affected flying. Mine was eventually five days.

I was accompanied by "B" Squadron friends, Fred McCullan and Frank Cowling. A lovely day in July 1952, which was at first spoiled by an altercation with an SIB Sergeant (mentioned later) but never-the-less a great relief to be away from the routine in the line. USAF Sky Master aircraft were used and I found myself as the senior passenger in charge of the flight. The first duty was to nominate six passengers from the rear to move forward to sit on the floor during take-off. It was announced that a Sky Master required a steel support rod propping up the high tail when on the ground. If weight wasn't forward, it tipped up, tail down! Soon in flight and heading east, Mount Fuji, the well-publicised volcano was clear to see and following a repeat performance of shifting the passengers for landing and we were in Tokyo for afternoon tea. A Japanese barracks had been taken over for Commonwealth troops and buildings had been chosen as Officers', Warrant Officers', Sergeants' and Soldiers' Messes. There was a process of cleansing to be experienced. All clothing off, shower and then collect a complete outfit of Jungle Green uniform and underclothing. Our badges of rank were permanently attached to a Brassard complete with U.N. badge. It was placed over the sleeve and secured by the epaulette. The sound of a toilet flushing gave me the greatest reminder of what I had missed! Then to the Mess rooms, white table cloths and service by Japanese girls. Had I died? Heaven is sometimes made up of the most trivial things. Ibitsu Camp was a short taxi ride to the Ginza in the centre of the city and we couldn't wait. A very necessary aid to driving in Tokyo was the horn, the driver kept one hand on it all the time. The noise of hundreds of horns was a cacophony of deafening sound but different and acceptable. Traffic, six lanes wide through high buildings re-echoed tenfold.

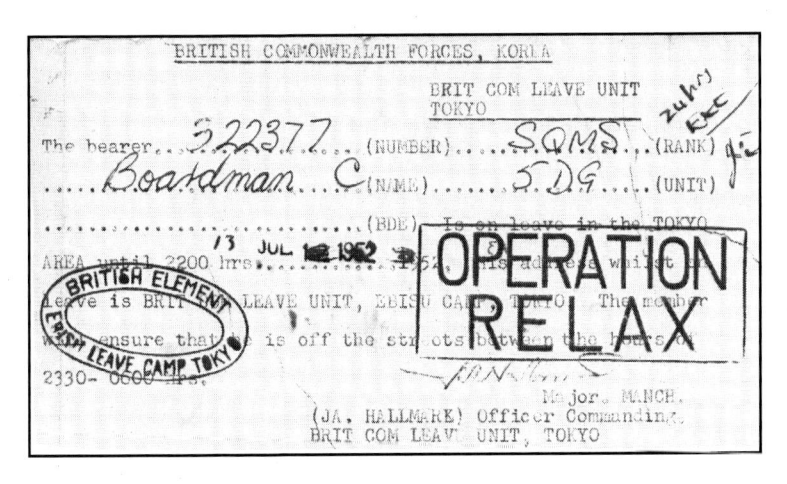

## TRACKS IN KOREA

I cannot remember the sequences of visits but it included a large store, a market which displayed and sold insects which looked like cockroaches and the smell of mysterious spices and herbs. The first night was an early retreat to sample clean sheets. Day one was recommended by the Australian staff to be a trip to a Turkish bath, and indeed it was a dream. Into a sweatbox, passed glasses of ice cold beer which produced sweat galore (some of it mixing with the beer!). Towelling by the attendants and then onto a couch for a massage. I noticed that the owners thought it necessary to display warnings, "Do not interfere with the attendants". A petite girl pulled and manipulated hands, feet and all manoeuvrable parts and then trampled on me. She looked at my bitten and damaged finger nails and called other girls to look. One spoke reasonable English and said "You have frostbite!" I went along with that although temperatures were in the eighties. Haircut and shave followed and it was into the streets. I thought it wise to buy presents to send home before our meagre pay ran out. I bought an eggshell green tea service and toys. Packing and dispatch was included in the cost. Later I bought other small items but by day three had spent-up. I was considering taking them back to Korea until we returned to the UK. A New Zealander who had accompanied us offered to send them for me and I parted with them without even remembering his name. All arrived home later. Should he ever read this book, please accept my deepest thanks. There were Women's' Voluntary Service (WVS) trips to various places of interest. It all came to an end on the third day, or we expected it to but flying conditions grounded the aircraft and we were without cash. The Australian Mess Sergeant begged us to stay in camp and attend the opening of a new Mess. As an attraction he said, "There are a number of American WAACS (Women's' Army Corps) invited and we have a band and all drinks are free! Visions of shapely blonds were dashed when a number of very over weight buxom girls arrived but never-the-less a fitting conclusion to a memorable stay.

P.S. The Tea-set was never used but still exists on a shelf in a granddaughter's house!

To add some further light relief I tell of a minor incident in the life of a Squadron Quartermaster Sergeant.

During one of my daily visits which included Lieutenant 'Micky' Fane's troop in support of the Norfolk Regiment, I was wearing my heavy wool pullover, dyed green. The infantry regiments had been informed that our officers were now wearing green pullovers but not that later this honour had been approved for our Warrant Officers and Sergeants. As I arrived, the Regimental Sergeant Major leapt from his bunker and delivered a salute worthy of a Queen's Birthday Parade. RSM Gilchrist was ex Irish Guards! I had no time to think and I thought it would embarrass him if I enlightened him. I was half hidden under the canopy of the Jeep, without hesitation I returned the salute and in the best impersonation of an officers accent that I could muster replied, "Good morning Mr Gilchrist, lovely day". The driver almost burst and I told him to drive on. This became a daily routine and the longer it went on, the more difficult it was to rectify it. I knew the Norfolks were about to be withdrawn and played the charade out. Just before they departed I received a message from my own RSM, that there was an invite for a number of our sergeants to attend a drinks party in the bunker serving as their Sergeants' Mess. He had nominated me to represent 'B' Squadron. I had to explain that if he didn't want an internal eruption within lines I was definitely a non-starter. It would take me a further ten years to achieve this honoured position in the 'Skins' but it may have been longer had the deception been discovered!

*Colonel Michael Anstice then recalls*

We devised a way of making distilled water as the commodity became scarce. Whether it was really fit for purpose I never knew, but it exercised our brains. I've often wondered if my memory isn't playing tricks, but two events are worth a mention, and Trooper Ron Marks, my gunner says they did happen. The first, we spotted a Chinaman leaving his dugout and presumably making his way to the latrine. We fired HE at him, missed and he waved to us. This continued for several days – we continued to miss and always got the wave. I hope he survived. The other was finding at dawn the fresh footprints of a Chinese patrol close to our troop position. Someone was always on watch during the night with head out of the turret and on net but we saw and heard nothing.

When in support of the 1st Norfolks, Hubert Holden, (Company Commander) and I waited for the standing patrols to return and then made our way through the minefields to the banks of the Samichon in no-mans land and put up duck. I can't remember if we ever shot anything, but the expeditions were the subject of an article in the Field Magazine. Although an easy shot for the Chinese they never bothered us!

Rats were always a problem. In one particular 'basha' they would run over me in my sleeping bag. Sometimes they would have battles on the floor leaving blood and fur behind. In reserve under Gloucester Hill the officers' mess tent ceiling was lined with cloth. We could see the rats' footprints and had great sport with our revolvers.

During a spell of air activity over the Chinese side a Sea Fury (a Spitfire modified to operate from an aircraft carrier) turned and made its way back heading straight for us, passing only a few feet above us. It crashed out of sight, but I could see the pilot dead in the cockpit. I think it had succumbed to small arms fire. Fifty years later when visiting the Commonwealth Cemetery in Pusan I noted the long list of RN lieutenants on a memorial. My father, as 5th Sea Lord, was in charge of the Naval Air Arm during the Korean War. I wish I had known of the heavy casualties at that time and could have asked for an explanation.

The First Sea Lord, when visiting the Regiment witnessed a demonstration shoot by the son of the 5th Sea Lord. The Chinese did not return fire.

REST AND RECUPERATION

My silver ½ pint Christening mug hung from the turret hatch handle. When Colonel Carr came to visit he was offered tea in this mug. Later I learned that RSM Chun gave my troop sergeant a ticking off for allowing the troop leader to serve tea to the Commanding Officer in a dirty old mug.

When taking over a troop position from David Rowat we stupidly allowed the sun to catch the talc (map case cover) on our map boards. A Chinese mountain gun opened up on us which led to an undignified scramble for cover. 3 RAR stood on the ridge cheering encouragement.

Carole Carr entertaining the troops. November 1952.

167

# A MOMENT OF GLORY WHICH FAILED
by the editor

There were many who deserve a special mention because of their outstanding devotion to duty. I have selected three. Sergeant "Jim" Gibson, "B" Squadron cook sergeant, who had four trained cooks and half a dozen Korean boys who worked for their food and accommodation in a primitive basher. He had inherited the nickname "Gibbo the Gook", Jim had served a long apprenticeship in Germany and frequently provided a gourmets delight at regimental functions. Those talents came to the fore in the late summer of 1952. The Squadron Leader had taken all officers and crew commanders to view new positions which we were about to occupy. I was the senior rank left to guard the camp at the base of Gloucester Hill. I was informed that the Commanding Officer wanted to speak to me on the land line. "Where is your squadron leader?" he enquired. I replied that he had taken a reconnaissance party to view new positions. "Well, I hope he remembers that an Admiral is visiting him today and will require lunch!" I assured him that he couldn't have forgotten that but knowing the concern Major Mike had for getting things right, I had my doubts. It could have never registered and in any case he was slightly deaf. The party was out of touch by radio. I ran to the marquee used as the officers' mess and asked the staff if they knew of the visit. There was a blank look which increased my concern. Jim Gibson was my next target. "We have a party of VIPs about to arrive requiring lunch," I informed him. "What can you do?" "No problem," he replied, "bags of bully beef, beans and a nice bit of steak!" On my way back to my tent I saw in the distance, a convoy of rather smart Jeeps approaching. I was about to entertain the Navy in the officers' mess at their expense and had to

# A MOMENT OF GLORY WHICH FAILED

think up a story to cover the delay. I was much relieved to see another convoy close behind the first group and they arrived within minutes of each other. I never enquired whether there was a plan, nobody asked me how the very tasty meal had been prepared and I certainly wasn't invited! I had been scuttled!

On another occasion Jim Gibson asked me to get him a bottle of whisky from the Sergeants' issue of a bottle a month - he had a liaison with an American who would supply him with a complete Calor Gas Field Kitchen. I obliged and it came complete with spare canisters. "Jim" wasn't just a cook!

My other selected personality of distinction was Sergeant Jimmy Myers who had served with me since 1942. He was in the Royal Army Ordnance Corps, who provided specialist mechanics and later became Royal Electrical and Mechanical Engineers and I a young Lance Corporal in the Reconnaissance Squadron. The "Fitters" worked long and often under dangerous conditions and Jimmy had come to my rescue many times. In Korea he took a great pride in keeping our sixteen Centurions road worthy, and together with his great friend Ron Teague, the gun fitter, they kept engines and equipment in top condition. This was particularly necessary to keep our second-in-command, "Bill" Garnett happy. His Jeep and tank had to be perfect at all times. There was a moment when both had something wrong. Mike Tomkin enjoyed stirring Bill up and said, "I understand that both your vehicles are off the road?" There was an indignant snort, Major Mike turned to me and said quietly, "When the Garnetts and the Kettles come to power we will see some sparks!" These memories I cherish.

The Myers 'Rocket'. provided permanent hot water.
Fitter troop Sgts Myers and Teague.

# AN INFANTRY PATROL REPORT BY THE ROYAL AUSTRALIAN REGIMENT

The following report is typical of a night patrol carried out by Infantry Regiments of the UK, Australia and Canada. It outlines the stress and danger of patrols negotiating set routes in the dark and dependent upon armoured support firing on pre-arranged targets. It is also a tribute to the assistance I have been given by the New South Wales Branch of the RAR Association.

"The situation was indeed grim for the battered survivors of a patrol pinned down on the frozen slopes of Hill 355 – a feature better known to the Diggers as 'Little Gibraltar' – just after midnight of 25th January 1953.

The Chinese dispersed and the survivors were able to withdraw back to the Battalion position. Bomber Terry, who had been wounded earlier in action, was never seen again. Consideration was later given to awarding him the Victoria Cross, but because his heroics were not witnessed by an officer, he was later instead Mentioned in Despatches. By any standards the trench raid had been a debacle – as the sun rose on 25th January, of the 30 men who ventured out into the gloom of No Man's land at 19.00hrs just the night before, 16 were missing. The soldiers that took part and listed their fates, Lt Smith commanded 12 men, Lance Corporal MacKay, 11 men and Sergeant Morrison went forward with 4 other men.

The Patrol Action report continues: "The patrol moved out as a whole for the first 1000 yards when Lt Smith's party was put down at a predetermined point. The remainder continued a further 1000 yards where Corporal MacKay's party took up position. Sergeant Morrison and his snatch party of 4 proceeded a further 600 yards to the objective.

On arrival at the objective, Sergeant Morrison put his party to ground along an embankment running immediately beside the enemy trench line. He then immediately jumped into the trench and was challenged twice by enemy picquets. These two, who appeared to be the only enemy in the vicinity, opened fire, so the Sergeant killed them. Immediately following this enemy automatic fire opened up from very close at hand. Having returned the fire the Sergeant's group withdrew quickly along their withdrawal route for a distance of 30 yards and called down tank support on the enemy position.

At this point a Chinese patrol of at least platoon strength engaged Lt Smith's party of 13 men. The report states: "A fierce fire fight started on the feature occupied by Lt Smith's group and large numbers of enemy were seen moving in the area".

Empty handed, Sergeant Morrison's 'snatch group' which included Bomber Terry as its signaller – rejoined Corporal MacKay's party of 12 men and they moved towards the fire fight ... within 200 yards they encountered 20 Chinese troops moving towards Lt Smith's position.

Sergeant Morrison's men took up firing positions and allowed the enemy to approach.

"The enemy were taken by surprise and were killed without opening fire", the report states. "The enemy when hit, fell in a number of cases, on the troops actually firing".

The fire from Lt Smith's location dying down, the Chinese switched their attention to Sergeant Morrison's party of 17 Diggers. By this time the Chinese strength had grown to at least two companies and smaller groups of enemy were seen moving around the area.

Sergeant Morrison decided to move to high ground which led back to A Company's position but when he reached it another group of 6 Chinese approached. With the larger group of Chinese closing from the rear, the Diggers were effectively surrounded. Decisive action

# AN INFANTRY PATROL

was needed – Sergeant Morrison and Corporal Frank MacKay moved forward and killed the 6 Chinese blocking their path on the ridge line in hand-to-hand fighting.

Sergeant Morrison's group quickly reorganised and moved forward but it was attacked by platoon-sized groups on two occasions on their right flank and once from the rear.

The report states: "These attacks were quickly broken up by immediate counterattacks with Owen gunners personally led by Sergeant Morrison in the first two instances and by Pte (Bomber) Terry in the case of the attack from the rear".

The aggressive action by the Diggers had broken the Chinese attacks and temporarily dispersed the demoralised survivors, but going head-to-head with a well-armed and motivated force more than almost 5 times your number was always going to be costly.

"During these attacks the groups that originally consisted of 18 (this may not be correct – a post war inquiry found that Sergeant Morrison had 4 men in his snatch party, and Corporal MacKay was left in charge of 11 men, which means that there were 17 Diggers in the second group) suffered 3 missing in action, 3 stretcher cases, 5 walking wounded", the Patrol Action report states.

"Despite this high percentage of casualties it is considered that the aggressive action on the part of Sergeant Morrison and his group was entirely responsible for the successful evacuation of all wounded.

"This action so disorganised the enemy ... that they disengaged and withdrew whilst the patrol group was still 500 yards from their Company localities. This allowed the last part of the withdrawal to be completed without interference".

Among the missing was the decisively brave Bomber Terry.

Dr O'Neill expands on Bomber Terry's action in the official history:

"Morrison led two charges against the flank attacks and Private Terry, who had been wounded earlier in the night, led another against the attack from the rear".

"Terry charged into a group of 20 Chinese, hurling grenades and firing his Owen gun. The Chinese stopped short and dispersed, but Terry was not seen again".

None of Lt Smith's party made it back to the A Company position that morning and it was assumed they had all been killed or captured. However, at about 13.30 hrs on 25th January 1953, three survivors – Privates' TJ Whiting, DM Murray and C Gale – arrived back at A Company's position. Debriefing of these men, which was the sole source of first-hand information of Lieutenant Smith's party, disclosed that the initial fire fight as heard by Sergeant Morrison's' group was occasioned by a platoon-sized attack against this group, the Patrol Action report reads.

"This attack was repulsed but was immediately followed by a further attack thought to have been of company strength launched from 3 directions. It was after this attack that Lieutenant Smith ordered the withdrawal of his group. However, he (Lieutenant Smith) and 4 others (Privates' Jack Saunders, Whiting, Murray and Gale) were the only ones seen to move. As the party withdrew, Lieutenant Smith was seen to be hit by a concussion grenade. The 3 men lay up well in enemy territory all night and began their journey back in early morning. The fourth man (Pte Saunders – Missing Believed Killed) was apparently killed or captured by the enemy".

The cost had been high, but Sergeant Morrison later estimated the doom patrol had killed at least 80 Chinese soldiers, apart from those killed by heavy mortar and artillery fire, which continued after the first lot of survivors returned. Heavy Chinese artillery fell on 3RAR's positions, killing 2 Diggers and wounding 2 more.

For the action Sergeant Morrison was awarded the Distinguished Conduct Medal and Lance Corporal MacKay the Military Medal. The Australian Commander of the 28th Commonwealth Brigade, Brigadier Thomas Daly and Lieutenant Colonel Hughes considered recommending Pte Terry for the Victoria Cross but there were not sufficient witnesses to document his undisputed bravery to meet the stringent requirements of the hallowed award.

## AN INFANTRY PATROL

Pte Terry was Mentioned in Despatches (later declared posthumous), as was Private CY Hales, who was one of the few members of Lance Corporal MacKay's group to finish the patrol unscathed. Their Association Secretary adds; "Only too pleased to help former comrades in arms as we once again find ourselves comrades in arms in Afghanistan".

# PROPAGANDA

The pamphlets shown are but a few dropped by air over Communist lines or surreptitiously hung on the wire netting of our lines. They were kindly translated by a Korean relation of a neighbour, Mr. Martin Priestly.
The findings are interesting;

*Mr. Jonathan Wright says:*

These are anti-Korean War propaganda aimed at getting Chinese soldiers to lay down their arms because they are being manipulated by the Soviet imperialists.
The first picture speaks of Chinese soldiers and Mao Zedong being controlled by the Soviets and being forced to fight in the Korean War.
The second is a call to run away from Allied cannons because the Chinese will perish without a decent burial in the conflict which sees the Chinese soldiers in disarray and killing each other.
The third is a letter stating Soviet Imperialist designs and persuading the Chinese soldiers to stop fighting in the face of huge losses, especially losses due to friendly fire.
The fourth is another call for the Chinese soldiers to resist Soviet Imperialism.
The writing is all in Chinese characters which were the only written form of language for Koreans (mostly for aristocrats) before the 1400s despite the fact that spoken Korean was very different from Chinese language. The Korean alphabet was created in the 15$^{th}$ century and has been recognized as one of the most scientific alphabets/written languages. People in Korea still use Chinese characters, but our own

PROPAGANDA

Korean alphabet is dominant now. I can only recognize a few Chinese characters, I am afraid. It seems to me that the images and writings on them mainly talk about Chinese involvement in the Korean War. The first image shows a Chinese soldier being pushed into the war zone by the Chinese government which is in turn pushed by the Russian. I was able to read several characters on that one. The other ones also talk about Chinese, but not Korean as much, it makes me wonder whether they were made by some sort of organization opposing Chinese involvement? You know the Koreans and the US-backed international troops were winning the war and the entire Korean peninsula was under our control before the massive Chinese involvement. It was such a shame. Had the Chinese (and Russians) stayed away, we could have had a united Korea. Signed "Yee"

The last was sent home by the editor in 1952 and translated by a friend. It is self-explanatory!

The first of these was from them to us and was left on the wire in front of our lines.

**SAFE CONDUCT PASS**

**THIS CERTIFICATE GUARANTEES GOOD TREATMENT**

*James A. Van Fleet*
JAMES A. VAN FLEET
COMMANDING GENERAL
UN FORCES IN KOREA

생명 보장

Above is a safe conduct leaflet of a type now being dropped over North Korean and Chinese troops opposing you. As indicated, it is a pledge of good treatment on our part to those of the enemy who can break away from Communist supervision in their units and come over peacefully. Other leaflets instruct such enemy troops, for their protection and yours, to: Desert their units at night; destroy their weapons; come over to our lines in daylight and along main routes or open country; come with their hands up and fingers extended. Air and ground loudspeakers repeat promises of good treatment. Word as to the type of treatment actually received gets back rapidly and largely determines whether the next man fights or surrenders. Therefore YOU can help YOURSELF by giving enemy troops every reasonable opportunity to surrender and by feeding them, treating them well and allowing them to keep their personal property. REMEMBER, the more of them who give themselves up, the less you will have to fight.

PROPAGANDA

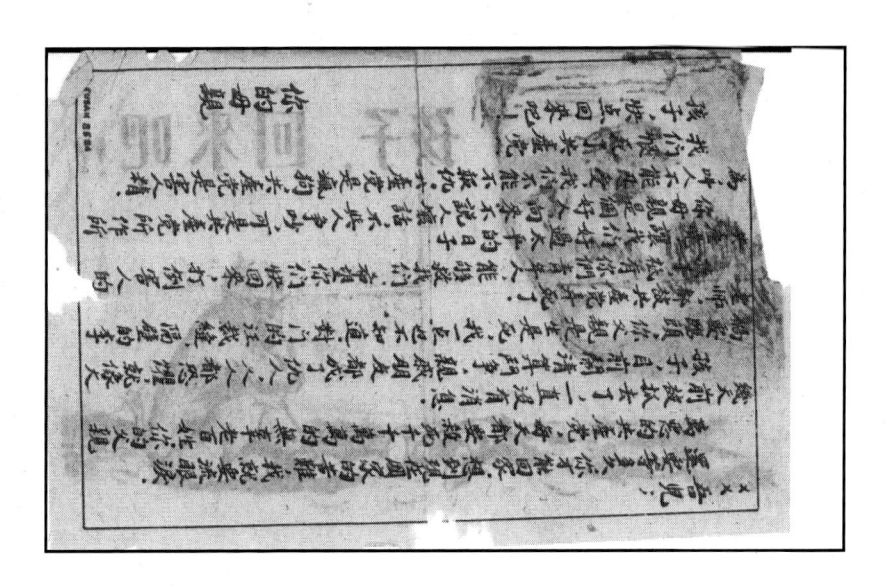

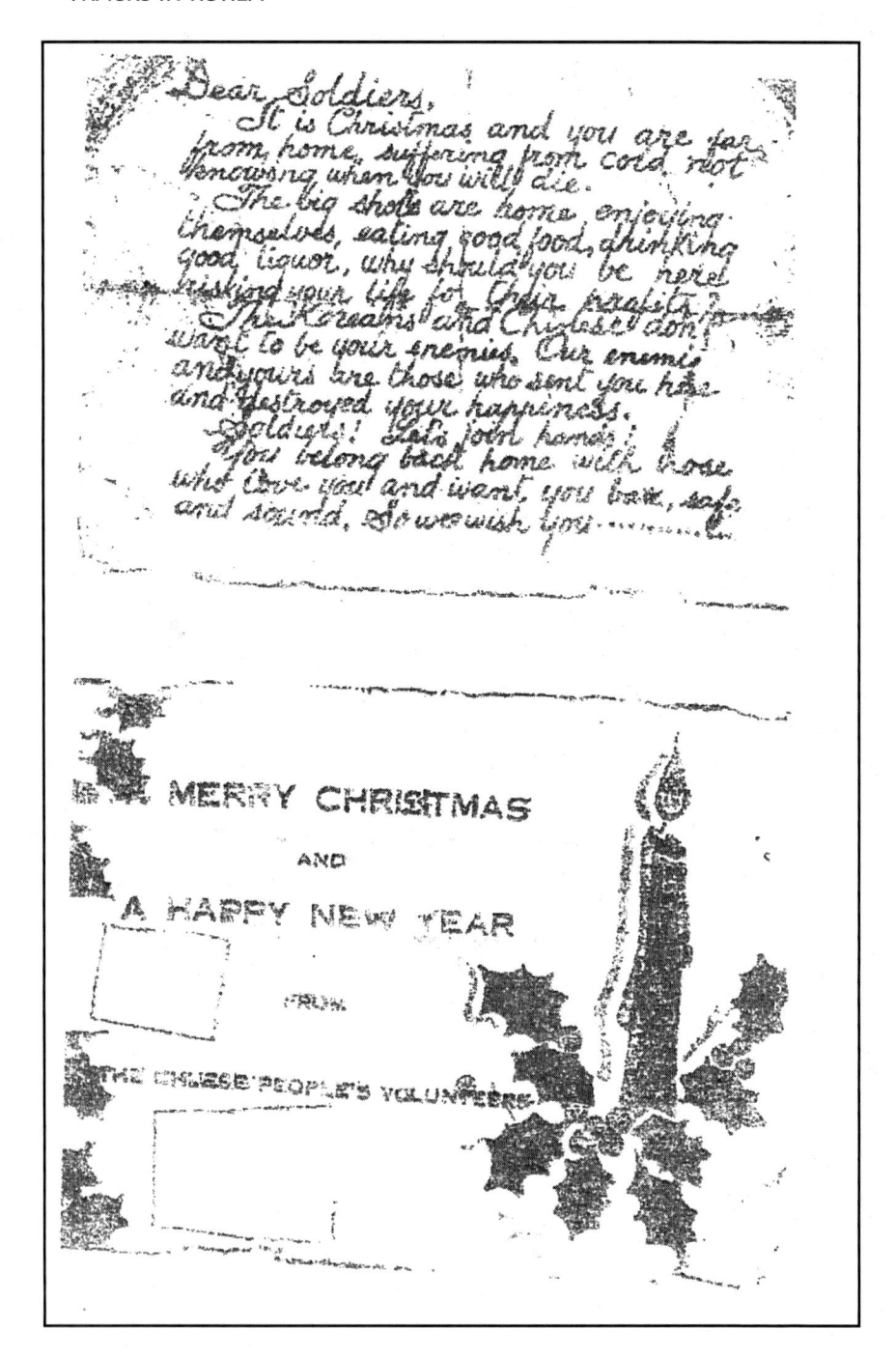

> Dear Soldiers,
> It is Christmas and you are far from home, suffering from cold, not knowing when you will die. The big shots are home, enjoying themselves, eating good food, drinking good liquor, why should you be here risking your life for China profits? The Koreans and Chinese don't want to be your enemies. Our enemies and yours are those who sent you here and destroyed your happiness. Soldiers! Let's join hands! You belong back home with those who love you and want you back, safe and sound. So we wish you........

**MERRY CHRISTMAS**

**AND**

**A HAPPY NEW YEAR**

FROM

THE CHINESE PEOPLE'S VOLUNTEERS

# PROPAGANDA

### SAFE CONDUCT PASS DROPPED OVER CHINESE LINES
### TRANSLATION

My Dear Son,

How long do I have to wait before you come back. Whenever I think of the crisis of the country, my tears stream down. Those evil communists! They kill thousands of innocent citizens every day. Your father was snatched a few days ago and up till now there is no news.

Dear child, their fighting for revenge now makes our relatives and friends enemies. Everybody is scared as if something dreadful is going to happen now. Whether your father is still alive or dead I don't know but the tailor 'Wong' and teacher next door have all been killed by Communists.

Dear child, it is only you young people who can save us. I hope you will come back soon and revolt against the Communists and let us live in peace.

Your mother never speaks ill about others, nor does she quarrel but what the communists have been doing I cannot control my feelings any longer. We must avenge communists. Dear child, come back quickly.

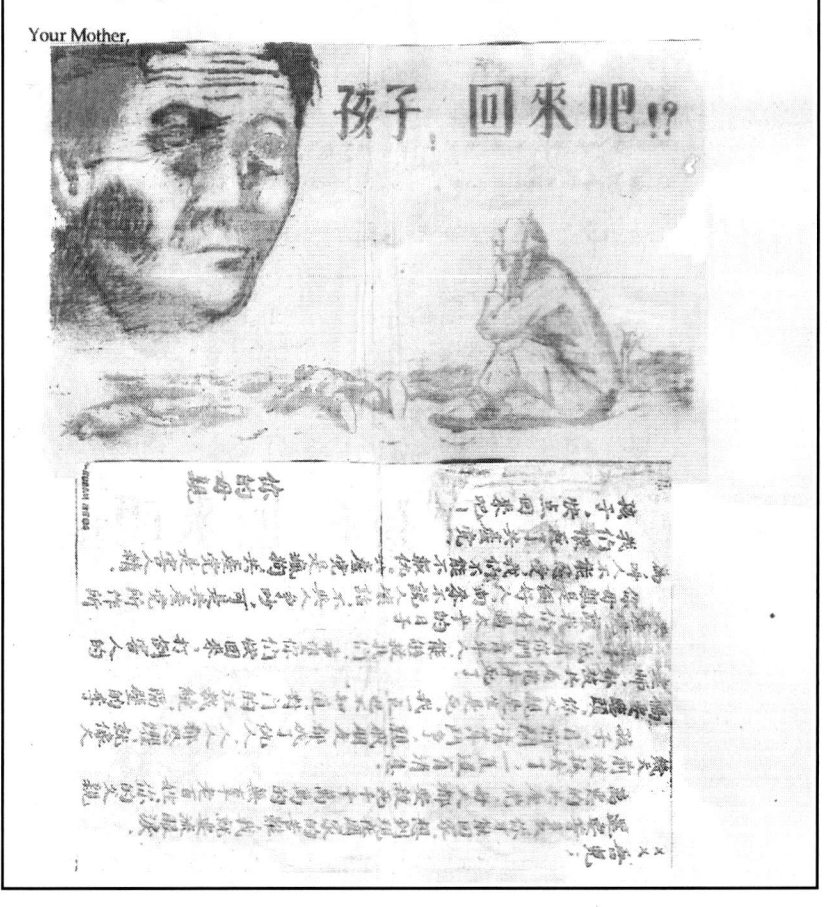

Your Mother,

炮兵掩護，
總是有的！
聯合國士兵隨時
有炮兵的掩護！

你現在制止你們向着被你們自殺害
澤東這們兄弟們你那由着冒痛的你們又用你
單是個你這是看中你們自自看到此們你已天上
們了經當們看看這他見殺炮炮
同你從不合上這此們人兵兵
俘得不自你們是早了上跟來
虜自細住知打已看你炮前
到細自道盡經見們兵同
國想你殺的了了的打國
人一們自你殺手軍的炮
不想要已要上了隊
會吧相的我了射你用了
在打信能們用手
打了我想個們的殺你兵回自
死吧們能炮你打來已己
你將夠兵是見下你們
們國被能的幹看了們看
歸的死大班殺部見關
队伤亡大的
能你到前進
毛夠們合白馬，才能呢？
的軍隊吧

PROPAGANDA

# THE PRICE OF PEACE
A tribute to the late Sergeant Harry Cookson.

Harry Cookson with the 8th Hussars.

# THE PRICE OF PEACE, A TRIBUTE TO HARRY COOKSON

Editorial

Were it necessary to justify the production of this Anthology, the fate of Harry Cookson would have provided the answer.

In 1951 Harry had been serving in Germany with the 10th Hussars. He volunteered to transfer to the "Skins". He was sent to Korea with our advance party in October 1951 and had little or no contact with the regiment. On arrival he was allocated to one of the Squadrons of the 8th Kings Royal Irish Hussars and became our first casualty. He sustained gunshot wounds to both legs, a bullet having entered one leg and lodged in the other. He also sustained shrapnel wounds. No doubt the normal casualty procedure was carried out by the 8th Hussars but we were at sea somewhere between the UK and Korea and Harry was unknown to us, the 10th Hussars had no part to play in it as Harry had been transferred to the 5th Royal Inniskilling Dragoon Guards and the 8th Hussars who were preparing to hand over to us would have treated his injuries as minor. They had no one to inform. A further problem was caused when it was decided to amputate his leg below the knee. His departure to the UK had been delayed because a party of senior officers took priority on the flight and gangrene set in, resulting in further surgery to remove the leg almost to the thigh. Meanwhile, his family had been informed that he had been killed in action, his mother was distraught. The police had misinterpreted the casualty telegram. Harry had become a "Martial Orphan".

In 1955, I was on leave at my wife's home in Northumberland and I met a young sergeant wearing 10th Hussar badges. Having been originally a 10th Hussar myself I made myself known. He was "Billy" Cookson. He told me of his brother and that he had been serving with our advance party but evacuated prior to our arrival. He was living nearby. I visited him and heard his story. We corresponded for some time but we lost contact because of my wanderings and his move to Cheltenham at some time. While en-route to re-visit Northumberland, during the proof-reading of this book, General Henry Woods commented that he thought there were still unknown stories and had I any other ideas. I had none to offer, all memory of Harry Cookson had been erased over the previous 56 years. Then, in 2011 we were called back to Northumberland for a family occasion. We had booked into a Guest House in Newbiggin and as the Satnav guided us in I recognised the area visited in 1955 and realised that if Harry was still living, he certainly had a story to relate. One of the visits we intended to make was to one of my wife Joan's friends from teenage years, who we knew had lived in Newbiggin for most of her life. I asked her whether she remembered Harry. "Oh yes", she replied but had not seen him for years. She knew of a contact who was related and would enquire. This resulted in a phone number awaiting us when we returned in the evening. Before I could use it, a cousin of Harry's by marriage, phoned me. She knew that Harry had been offered employment in Cheltenham and that he, his wife Kathy and brother Billy had died some years earlier. It seemed the end of the story except that I had contact with the local editor of a monthly newsletter circulated to Geordies, worldwide. I wrote an appeal for information. This resulted in a cousin by marriage living in the Nottingham area contacting me. She in turn had contact with one of Harry's daughters, Jill Holder, living in Cheltenham delighted to help. Harry hardly ever talked of his problems but he had joined the Royal British Legion, the British Korean Veterans and had been assisted to return to Korea in 1983. He had been treated in Roehampton and due to the shortness of the stump, had been taught to walk with crutches. Harry made many friends during his rehabilitation, including the technicians who applied plaster of paris. They made him a leg from it and it served as a prototype for a metal leg which lasted him for the rest of life. To add to his injuries he developed Parkinson's' Disease which he endured for the last ten years of his life. He never complained and died aged 72 in 1998. He had become a superintendent with General Electric, had a happy marriage and raised two daughters.

Readers may feel that the system failed him, including my own intervention in 1955, but at that time Regimental Associations were strictly Old Comrades and members paid a subscription, a secretary was employed and operated from his home. It was headed by the Colonel of the Regiment with a voluntary committee, mainly to arrange reunions at our three areas where the regiment had been stationed; York, Colchester and Northampton. Minimal financial assistance was available. In 1961 government backing provided a building with a retired officer, staff and regimental museum. It was linked to the serving regiment, the title changed to the "The Regimental Association" and care and assistance with newsletters provided. There are still criticisms. In 1955, Harry, having not joined our Old Comrades Association, would have been unknown. He probably had his own friends and corresponded by letter but Jill doesn't remember him having any contact. This report will contribute to any family research and they may feel proud of Harry Cookson. (Any reader who witnessed the action which resulted in Harry Cookson's wounding may be able to complete this story).

# SUMMING UP

If the reader is feeling a little battle weary and bored with the numerous thrusts and counter thrusts, spare a thought for the men in the front line. The routine was to 'stand to' an hour before dawn in readiness to counter any attack from the enemy patrols which had crossed the no-man's land during the hours of darkness. As stated in the Chinese report, the Chinaman was trained to take up a camouflaged position and lay perfectly still for hours and then strike when we stood down. There was a wire entanglement in front of our positions but these could be breached. Sometimes propaganda pamphlets were hung on this wire to prove that a patrol had been close during darkness. A constant watch had to be maintained. Those serving in the control positions (CP) could move about quite freely until a sudden artillery attack was made. To give some relief from the continued strain, various initiatives developed. Some took an interest in the wildlife. A Golden Oriole was often seen flying across the valleys, Swallows became very tame during the nesting season and built nests in the bunkers constructed for the crews and only feet from the occupants. During a change of squadrons, a swallow had built its nest in the canopy of a vehicle used as a machinery wagon. To avoid disturbing it, the vehicle was left until the nest was abandoned. The thousands of frogs mating in the paddy fields made a continuous croak, sounding like a vehicle with snow grips on the move. There was an abundance of Praying Mantis (large grasshoppers). The large black ants loved them. Some fun was obtained by killing one, waiting for an ant to find it, watch it report back and come forward, cut it into manageable pieces and drag it away. Artificial obstructions could be created and the sacrifices made to cross water could only be admired. Rats and mice were rife

# SUMMING UP

and fed well among the empty tins. They carried the nasty Songo Fever bug which remained with the rat when alive but left if it died. A dead rat in the sand bagged walls of a bunker had to be avoided. This brings a memory of my much admired Squadron Leader Major Mike Tomkin. I had obtained a battery operated welfare radio and it served us well to keep in touch with the world and usually updated Commonwealth Division newsletter, 'The Crown News'. I had tuned in for the Forces programme transmitted from Kure, Japan, and was listening to the report on the Test match, England v Australia. The sun was suddenly blotted out by the figure of my leader who asked, "What's the score?" He was a good cricketer himself so I gave him an update. "Not cricket", he replied, "Rats". It was his polite way of reminding me that rat destruction was in progress and I would be better employed supervising it. The solution was to smear clothing with anti-mite fluid daily and organise a rat destruction day periodically. Petrol was poured into every hole visible, men stood by with shovels; matches lit the petrol which popped up in other holes. As the rats came out they were clobbered. The fields were a breeding ground for mosquitoes which carried the malaria virus. A Paludrine tablet had to be taken daily. I don't think anyone caught it but during the following summer when serving in Egypt, many went down with it and caused a panic. Egypt was not a malaria country. We then learned that we should have continued the tablet once a day for a further six months.

# A RAT STORY
by Don Pooley

It has been reported elsewhere about the problem with rats inhabiting the dugouts and bashas in the front line and reserve locations. I had a problem when the Squadron were in reserve in Gloucester Valley with a rat or rats trying to nibble through whatever they fancied in my basha. In my troop were two talented National Servicemen, Lance Corporal Geoff Beighton and Lance Corporal Alan Goforth. Geoff had just finished his apprenticeship as a cabinet maker before being called up and Alan was just very clever with anything involving the use of wood. I asked them if they could make a rat trap. They constructed a wooden tunnel, made out of the boxes the bottled beer came in. It was approximately 12 inches long and 6 inches square with open ends. On one end they fixed some wire mesh, the other end had a hinged door cantilevered with a heavy piece of rock on the top so that when it closed it was held tightly shut. The door had a handle connected via rubber bands to a wire with a hook dangling through the wire mesh. On the hook was the bait, the rats' favourite chocolate. The theory of the design was that the rat would be enticed through the door end, nibble the chocolate on the hook which would release the rubber band and the door would shut, held in place by the heavy stone. That night the trap was set on the ground about a foot away from where I was sleeping. During the night I was woken up by a large bang and shining a torch I was staring into the eyes of a very large rat. Bingo! The trap had worked. The next problem was keeping the thing quiet for the rest of the night so it was given a bit more chocolate. The next morning, with the news that we had a result, the lads gathered around and there followed a discussion of what to do with the rat. Drowning was the answer. Someone produced a large bucket of water and I think it was Alan who did the honours. He held the trap vertically with the wire mesh end at the bottom, the rat standing on its head. Alan plunged the whole trap into the bucket of water. The rat then summoned up every ounce of energy in its body, turned around, forced open the door, leapt out between the assembled companies and made good his escape up the hill. Maybe it deserved its freedom after all that effort.

There was a character named Trooper Hadfield. SSM Charlie Gower employed him as the operator of the incinerator. He was a one off and most units had one. The pit required took him days to dig out and line with empty ammunition containers. The first problem caused Charlie to explain to him that he wasn't a foreword thinking man in a manner which would have filled a swear box. Hadfield had forgotten to take something to climb on to get out of the hole! On the first big burn, ignited by an overdose of petrol, the flames caused the air to pass the end of the ammunition containers and exit in the same way as a church organ. He could vary the pipes and get different chords.

This effect was also used by an American Heavy Artillery Battery located beside us, when in one of the rest areas on the Imjin. By punching holes in a missile it created a variation of sound when fired. It all relieved the monotony of life for some. The same American Unit also provided us with something to think about. We were celebrating St. Patricks' Day and I went over and invited the Warrant Officers and Sergeants to come over to our Mess for a drink. There were about a dozen and each one brought a Private. We explained that the lower ranks had their own Mess. "That's OK Bud, they can join them", replied the Top Sergeant. "They are only here to carry us home!"

Some relief was created in the rear areas by levelling an area of Paddy by dragging a heavy iron bar to act as a grader. Basketball hoops were easily made by welding a strip of metal into a circle and attaching a string vest. We managed to construct a reasonable cricket wicket and tried to educate the Yanks but they were more successful in teaching us baseball. We learned a few tricks from them to improve

# TRACKS IN KOREA

our basketball too. There was a mobile cinema provided by the Army Kinema Corporation (AKC). A screen was set up in a suitable area where troops could sit on the banks to watch. This had to be at night of course and the beam of the projector was an attraction to mosquitoes. A few live shows visited. On one occasion I was surprised to see so many vehicles parked up and investigated; they were watching a show in a recess in the hillside and Larry Adler, the American mouth-organ wizard doing a turn!

In later years and while competing at Bisley with my friend 'Ginty' (SSM Bill Gilliland), we were collected by a wartime friend and taken to his pub in Thames Ditton. We were in uniform and immediately attracted the attention of the barmaid. She recognised our Korean medal ribbons and asked had we been there. We replied in the affirmative and she dashed to the rear shouting, "Hi darling, there are some friend of yours here". A tall shapely woman appeared and introduced herself as Hi Hazel, who was reputed to have the longest legs in show business. Don't worry if you have never heard of her, nor had we. We invited her to have a drink, she ordered a Pimms, which was not in our budget. We departed before she needed another.

The Mobile Bath Unit was a chance to move and have a spruce up, cold in winter but necessary. In summer we took advantage of the numerous streams which ran down the hillsides. There was also a laundry service which was quite efficient. One item not washable by normal standards was the sleeping bag. It was necessary in winter to sleep in your clothing or at least keep them in your bag to keep warm. Frequently it was necessary to keep boots on and not surprisingly the bag looked as though coal had been carried in it. As a precaution against lice a chemical called AL 63 was used lavishly. It has long been proclaimed dangerous to health and banned.

As an SQMS (Squadron Quartermaster Sergeant), I was in a far safer employment than I had been during World War II as a crew commander in the reconnaissance squadron, but there were moments of concern. I have chosen two.

As the appointed researcher, I have the advantage of knowing what others have written to avoid duplication which permits me to concentrate on the similarities of the war in Korea and Iraq and in the present war in Afghanistan, in which The Royal Dragoon Guards are currently involved. Already there have been casualties. The modern soldier has to face the same experiences of fatigue, irregular meals and sadness in the loss of close friends as those of the parent regiments have in previous years. The 4/7th Royal Dragoon Guards and the 5th Royal Inniskilling Dragoon Guards now operate under the title The Royal Dragoon Guards and under their motto 'Quis Separabit', (who shall separate us?). The opinion of some members of the public and some government ministers has been as it was in 1950, that we are involved in a war of little interest to ourselves. The Korean venture is not ended. Threats by the communist North to the Western civilisation in the South are as strong as ever. South Korea has progressed from a primitive rice growing country to become a leading international highly skilled industrial nation and taken its place in the world market of sport and trade. We can only hope that my theory that the history of the past being the best forecast for our future proves true. The Korean War contributed to the cessation of the spread of communism and to the collapse of the Soviet Empire. We must trust that our forces in Afghanistan will be rewarded in a similar way.

# A SAD FAREWELL
by the editor

My remaining memories of departure from the Land of the Morning Calm, come as a direct result of a sense of understanding with a Korean man in his mid-twenties, who I had taken over from my counterpart in the 8th Hussars.

On the night of arrival I, with my store man, "Paddy" Walsh found a place for our sleeping bags among the sea kitbags containing items not required in the frontline. I was awakened in the morning by the shouting of my 8th Hussars counterpart, who was most put out because "Charlie", as he was known, had given me priority access to the hot tea and a bowl of boiling water for washing. I was to learn that he was totally deaf but a great asset. Indeed he was. What he lacked in hearing was compensated fully in the faithful care and attention he gave not only me but the troops throughout the year. My every need was covered. Clothes washed, boots dried and cleaned, my stores immaculate.

He had been accompanying our predecessors since the initial outbreak of war in 1950. I could communicate with him perfectly. The days before and after were indicated by a wave of the hand to the left for yesterday, right, tomorrow and followed by any number of fingers to indicate the number of days. He issued a variety of daily needs to the troops, anything from boot laces, loo rolls and candles to paraffin oil for lamps and field dressings. All was understood perfectly. He had obtained spare clothing from departing units, ranging from a pair of pyjamas to a Dinner Jacket. He wore a black beret with cap badges of previous regiments displayed. He preferred to wear his pyjama trousers as a summer day dress!

His deafness was a problem, particularly if I didn't get up when he delivered the tea and water. He would storm in, grunting and gesticulating and take it away to reheat. No amount of shouting stopped him. It was the cause of a nasty accident. He was digging a trench around a store tent and intended to spray creosote in it to deter ants, rats, snakes and other nasties from crossing it. He had obtained a stirrup pump and was trying to spray the ground. He was very strong and I realised that the creosote was too thick. I ran towards him, predicting that the hose would be forced off the nozzle. I didn't predict that I would bear the full force of it in my face. I couldn't see, it was choking me and burning. Fortunately, the squadron medical orderly had heard the commotion and did exactly the right counter-action by dipping my head in clean water many times. Eyebrows burned, lips, nostrils all affected, I was taken to the Canadian Aid-post for treatment and recovered in a week.

On another drain digging operation I queried the depth of a trench round our stores. It was a hot, cloudless day with no signs of rain. The following day I quickly understood the reason, rain, which bounced of the dry earth and caused a heavy warm mist. We were in the Gloucester Valley rest area which became rapidly a quagmire. The Imjin River rose thirty-six feet (36) in twelve hours and put all our bridges in danger. The Chinese were quick to take advantage and threw anything from trees to rubbish into it from a point up river which piled against the scaffolding. Our tanks were used to fire high explosives at it to break it all up. A double rum ration was issued to all ranks for many days.

In mid-summer Charlie informed me that he was going to get married. We gave him some rations and other items. He had great delight in riding in the front of a truck and was fascinated by the pointers on the dash-board.

He accompanied the trucks returning empty beer bottles to the Brewery but found a market which exchanged them for other necessaries. Beds made from timber bound with telephone cable, chairs and other oddments. He also brought me a live chicken and rooster, a duck and a rabbit. We had a menagerie which travelled with us and was eventually handed over. They wandered about during the day and fed well. I did enquire of the 1$^{st}$ RTR as to what fate they had met and was sad to learn that they had been eaten. After the wedding, Charlie brought back a photograph. Hair very heavily oiled, DJ and bowtie, bride in a full white gown except that he was wearing his heavy boots Wet/Cold!

Not long after the marriage he failed to return from one of his trips and I supposed that he had other duties to attend to. Two weeks later a driver came to me very concerned. He had seen "Charlie" sitting on the roadside at a South Korean checkpoint with Chinese POWs. I set off immediately. He had been very badly beaten and was terrified. I remonstrated with the South Korean Guards who explained that as he couldn't speak their language they had thought him to be hostile. What his future would have been I hate to think. It was a happy "Charlie" who accompanied me back to our area.

In certain weather conditions, our New Zealand Artillery fired High "Proximity" fused high explosive shells which were intended to detonate above ground level for maximum effect. Cloud sometimes caused them to detonate above us. He couldn't hear it but the shock waves caused him to flinch. I tried to get him to sleep on the floor of the bunker but he preferred to take his chances.

As the day of departure approached I obtained an atlas and indicated to him where we came from and our next location on the Suez Canal. He understood but couldn't understand why he couldn't come with us. He was inconsolable. Come the day we walked together to the assembled vehicles but he wouldn't be put off, still intent on departing with us. My last sight of "Charlie" crying on the road-side, still fills me with sorrow. What did happen to my friend, "Lee Won Am?"

I have chosen my own experiences to enlighten the reader on events which affected those who served and their families during this troublesome period, particularly our families.

For those mothers and children who had no alternative to being

# A SAD FAREWELL

accommodated in the camp at Corsham, it was a very difficult time and for some it lasted until the Regiment returned to Catterick in January 1954.

In the October of 1952, married soldiers were contacted and informed of our pending move to the Suez Canal area to serve a further year. Again the family crisis was of great concern. The given solution then was that the families would be accommodated in Benghazi. It didn't take long to raise the question, "What was the advantage of having a family 600 miles away in another strange country. How often would we see them?" That was quickly abandoned. Only 18 families joined us in the Canal area and I was most fortunate in being one. It was an on-going problem for others. The National Servicemen need not have caused us any concern, they performed as well as any regular, and they were a tribute to British youth. One of my experiences emphasises this and had a happy outcome but might have been more serious. It concerned a young NSM named Trooper Fisher. He had joined the regiment just prior to departure and having some clerical experiences, was given the prestigious position as Squadron Clerk. Major Mike Tomkin treated him as a master would when correcting homework. On one occasion when I was in the sandbagged bunker used as an office, I witnessed one of these sessions. As Fisher left, Mike Tomkin added to his previous rebuke, "Fisher while you're correcting that, fix the map which has been minus a pin for a week, you may remember the old proverb. For the want of a nail the shoe was lost, the want of a shoe, the horse was lost, etc. You may be able to think of other suitable proverbs to fit the situation". To which Fisher replied, "Yes Sir, I can". There was a pause and he insubordinately replied, "More haste less speed". There was an eruption. I found it amusing but left with an ambition to, in some way, inflict a reprisal on this cheeky youth. My opportunity came one quiet summer evening when the mail arrived. There were no shell or mortar reports coming in and I said to Major Mike, "I'll go round the troops while it is quiet". "Take my jeep", he replied "and take a man with you". The unfortunate Fisher appeared. "Get your Sten-gun and get in the back", I said. The fear of the unknown was evident on his face and it gave me the satisfaction I desired. He said nothing during the bumpy, dusty journey. We arrived at the prominent feature known as 355, where a tunnel constructed of camouflage nets covered the approach to a long bulldozed track to the site of a troop of tanks overlooking the valley. The tactic was to go slowly through the nets to avoid a dust cloud. For some reason it didn't work and a salvo of shells came over, none hit the road, and most fell well down the hillside to the right. The next tactic was to stop in the areas protected by land on the winding track and vary the time, a quick dash to the next point in the hope that the enemy gunners misjudged the timing. There was another salvo but it didn't affect us. I was beginning to have a guilty feeling about Fisher but said nothing. The troop on the hill had watched our approach with interest and clapped as we arrived. A tin of beer and chat and we went off on the return, we received the same treatment. During one of the waiting periods, Fisher leaned forward and said, "I've got the hang of this 'Q'." "What are your findings?" I asked. "You're shitting yourself just like me, but you're not showing it", he replied. "How true", I admitted. It was just one small indication of the way those boys, some straight from school, established themselves.

There was another incident during the Korean conflict which I treated as a bit of a joke at the time but it could have had serious consequences. A tank crewman had been wounded and evacuated. Some bedding had been destroyed. It was my duty to replace it and recover what were designated War Office Controlled Stores, in this case a .38 revolver and a pair of binoculars. I returned to the Squadron HQ called a Control Point (CP), threw the revolver in its holster into the bunker which I shared with the Squadron Sergeant Major and once again left on the pleasant mission to collect mail. On arrival at Tactical HQ, I was informed that it had not arrived but was not far away. I had, on this occasion taken the Squadron Signal Sergeant. RSM Chun invited the Sergeant and I to share a tin of beer. The driver, Lance Corporal

# A SAD FAREWELL

Robin Kitt, a Czechoslovakian whose English was poor, appeared and informed me that his side lights didn't work and the return journey would be in the dark. There were varied areas of 'side lights only', and finally, 'no lights'. I told him to pack the headlights with cotton waste and make a small hole through it. The mail arrived and we set off to start the return journey. When we arrived at the no lights area all four of us had to lean out of the side of the Jeep to keep an eye on our position on the road as there were deep ditches on either side. The journey was in the end, uneventful. The following evening I returned to my bunker to find a Military Policeman who made himself known as a Special Investigator. He was sitting on my bed talking to the Squadron Sergeant Major. I thought it was a confidential matter and said I would return later. "No", he replied, "It's you I want to see". He questioned me on the previous evening's journey and asked me to confirm that I had collected a revolver from 355. I had had a drink at Tactical HQ. There had been a problem with lights. I eventually got him to tell me what the enquiry was about. Your vehicle was the only vehicle travelling on that road recorded at a check point and somebody had fired a shot from it and killed a cook of the Royal Norfolk Regiment. I was relieved and explained that if I wanted to shoot someone, I could use my own revolver, the night was so dark that we couldn't see the sides of the road let alone a man, and what was the Norfolk cook doing alone at night in the area? I also had three others in the Jeep who would verify this. This resulted in the Czechoslovakian driver being arrested, as a search of his personal items had revealed some pornographic photographs! I suggested that this was a very unjust method to obtain information. What I didn't know was that Robin Kitt in his limited English had said after a long and gruelling questioning, "So the Norfolk cook was pissed, got lost and was shot, there is a war going on". This was taken to be some form of confession. Two weeks later when about to board an aircraft for Tokyo at Seoul Airbase to enjoy 5 days Rest and Recuperation, the SIB Sergeant arrived for the same reason, I laughed and mocked, "How's the Norfolk cook affair going?" "Don't feel so cocky", he replied, "You are still the main suspect". Eleven years later when being questioned by a Brigadier during the process of being Security Vetted he came to the question, "Have you had any dealings with Communists?" I replied, "Yes, we had a few but most were mixed up with the trade unions and not taken very seriously". He then said, "What about Korea?" "Oh Yes, I replied, plenty of them there but I had little contact". "What about the incident involving the murder of a cook?" he asked. I was horrified that some form of record existed. I obtained a copy of my records later but could find no mention.

On a more humorous note I recall a day when the Chinese celebrated May Day by sending over 2000 rounds onto our front. When it had died down I ventured out to do my rounds but took the Squadron half-track which was armour plated. I had to pass the site of our American Artillery unit which was providing support for us. To my surprise, the camp was empty except for some tent cover and a four seated portable toilet. We had very primitive boxes with a hole cut out and I envied the Yanks their loo. When I returned, I notified my Squadron Leader and sought his permission to recover the super-loo. "Get a truck and bring it back here", he replied. No one ever came to reclaim it.

******

In gratitude for all that I owe to the regiment and those I have served with I bequeath this book to the Royal Dragoon Guards and all who have served in the founder regiments. It has been an honour.

> For everything there is a season, and a time for every matter under heaven:
> A time to be born, and a time to die;
> A time to plant, and a time to pluck up what is planted;
> A time to kill, and a time to heal;
> A time to break down, and a time to build up;

A time to weep, and a time to laugh;
A time to mourn, and a time to dance;
A time to embrace, and a time to refrain from embracing;
A time to seek, and a time to lose;
A time to keep, and a time to throw away;
A time to tear, and a time to sew;
A time to keep silence and a time to speak;
A time to love, and a time to hate;
A time for war, and a time for peace.

The camouflaged entrance to Hill 355.

There are many memories which have remained with me all these years. Korea in general is not a period that I or any others could have enjoyed. The co-ordinating of this book has compensated for it. A visit to the recently founded National Arboretum is a wonderful reminder to add to my two medals, the British Korean and United Nations Medal, but most of all a yellowing parchment headed, Commander-in-Chief's Certificate of Devotion to Duty and a letter from Trooper

## TRACKS IN KOREA

Fisher's father, thanking me for looking after his son during his tour of duty! Using my analogy of 'the history of the past being a guide to the future', beware of the men in dark suits in Whitehall. As soon as emergencies die down there will be a reduction in the Forces by disbandment, amalgamation and redundancy. Heed the words of a poem found scratched on a sentry box in Gibraltar, undersigned, 'From a Soldier'.

> "God and the Soldier, all men adore,
> In time of danger and not before
> When the dangers past and all things righted,
> God is forgotten and the Soldier slighted".

Had it been possible to accompany the reader with suitable music my choice would have been my favourite piece, 'Dances with Wolves'. The Korean War never had a signed peace treaty and it is doubtful that any veteran will live to witness it. It is not the end of a story but the alternative could have been other wars in the defence of democracy and probably greater loss of life. I consider it to have been a worthy cause.

It had been a full and active year but the regiment, whilst remembering with sorrow and pride their comrades who lie forever in South Korea and the amazing spirit of the Commonwealth Division, was not sad to be bound for the Canal Zone of Egypt.

# THE FINAL DAYS

Minor affrays involved the regiment during the remainder of November, both 'A' and 'B' Squadron supporting company raids by 1st Durham Light Infantry, 1st Royal Fusiliers, 1st Royal Australian Regiment and, beyond the Division right boundary, 1st Republic of Korea Division. Sporadic outbursts of shelling continued, and on 28 November an 'A' Squadron tank was hit by an 85-mm round fired from an enemy armoured vehicle. 'C' Squadron trained with 1st Duke of Wellingtons and 3rd Royal Australian Regiment, and ran conversion courses for Lord Strathconas' Horse who anticipated soon changing from Shermans to Centurions.

In 24th November the Commanding Officer of 1st RTR joined his advance party in the regimental area. Amongst many farewells, the joint church parade with 'B' Lord Strathcona's Horse on 30 November was probably the highlight. Afterwards presents were exchanged marking 'the end of our association but not we hope of our friendship'. On 8th December the main parties of 1st RTR, old friends from Detmold, arrived and went to squadron areas, taking over at first light 9th December. By lunchtime the regiment gathered at the Tokchong railhead and were soon trundling southwards by train through the snow-covered mountains. As the train began to move convulsively, a mighty cheer rose. Later the regiment had a snowball exchange with unsmiling South Korean Military Police at Taegu, before arriving very late at Seaforth Camp in Pusan. On 12th December with the regiment formed up in a hollow square, facing the Union Jack and with the regimental flag at half-mast in the United Nations Cemetery, our Padre, the Reverend DS Coey, conducted a moving memorial service to those on our Roll of Honour. In the background, fluttering in the cold breeze of a bright hard winters' afternoon flew the flags of all the countries represented in the UN Forces in Korea, while bugles of the Durham Light Infantry sounded Last Post and Reveille.

The regiment arose very early on 14th December, and by 10.00hrs embarkation on the 'Empire Halladale' was complete, with many out on deck listening to the American Army Band who marched to and fro on the quayside playing the 'St Louis Blues' with great gusto and élan. Local dignitaries, such as the Minister of Defence of South Korea and the American Port Commandant, accompanied by the Commanding Officer took their places on a dais in front of the flags of the United Nations. The Port Commander gave a resounding address, to which the Commanding Officer replied. Soon afterwards, the 'Empire Halladale' cast off and Pusan disappeared rapidly into the wintry haze astern.

*Captain John Hobart recalls 'the snowball incident'*

Late December 1952 and the Skins were in good cheer on the train to Pusan to catch the boat to Shandur with the promise of warmth and endless sunshine. The train pulled into a snow covered station for a routine stop and a lot of Skins with stiff joints and numb backsides, from the wooded seats, jumped on to the platform and the track for a stretch.

On the platform there were two smart looking US Military Policeman, who, resplendent in chromium plated helmets, caught the attention of the dismounted Skins. Snowballs were already being tossed back and forth among the Skins and it wasn't long before some snowballs were being lobbed toward the so called "Snow Drops", who reacted in a most un-seasonal way by drawing their "forty-fives" and ordering the snowball throwers to "Knock it off".

Word of the "Snow Drops" officious attitude went quickly down the train and a hundred more Skins poured off the train and began making snowballs. Clearly the MPs had not weighed up the odds of two "forty fives" against 600 battle-hardened Skins, still armed to the

THE FINAL DAYS

teeth, who did not take kindly to being ordered about by two fancily dressed MPs who had likely not been within a hundred miles of the front line. It was a Mexican stand-off.

The prize went to the Koreans, who scored a diplomatic coup in defusing the stand-off when their police and soldiers launched a full scale attack on the Skins who took up the challenge with gusto. The killjoy "Snow Drops" were forgotten in an instant. Both sides thoroughly enjoyed the snowball fight and the Skins returned to the train exhausted to wave a happy farewell to their Korean opponents.

*Footnote*

Reading a social history of the Koreans the writer discovered how similar they are to us Brits. When we were kids (there was no TV and the cinemas were closed on Sundays) our crowd would go to a disused quarry, divide into two teams and have a stone throwing battle. In the winter we would have great snowball fights. There was plenty of exercise and fresh air. In Korea, a village would arrange to have a stone throwing fight with a neighbouring village in which everyone- old, young, male and female- took part. In winter snowballs replaced the stones.

\*\*\*\*\*\*

A unique and remarkable year in the regiment's life was over. If there were any regrets at leaving Korea, they were because we were leaving the Commonwealth Division, every part of which was knit together by tremendous comradeship and spirit based on the symbol of the Crown. Throughout the year the regiment were well aware of the special debt of gratitude owed to the 'attached' Officers, NCOs and soldiers from other cavalry regiments, from the Royal Tank Regiment, the Royal Australian Armoured Corps, and the Royal New Zealand Armoured Corps who had been with us either throughout or for part of the year. Their loyalty and high sense of duty and their temporary but total identification with the regiment gave us an insight into the high standards of their own regiments and corps. They had taken their places in our tank crews with enthusiasm and high professional skill. The loyalty and devotion to duty of so many National Servicemen of the regiment, who voluntarily extended their service, deserves renewed praise.

The regiment suffered comparatively few casualties, mercifully light compared with some other campaigns; one officer and eight NCOs and soldiers were killed in action, and four soldiers died on active service. The wounded were excellently cared for and often transported so rapidly by helicopter to well-equipped hospitals that their wounds were being treated within minutes rather than hours. Seven officers and twenty NCOs and soldiers were wounded in action and nearly all returned fully fit to duty with the regiment. The Korean War, a struggle spluttering towards an armistice, differed from the North West Europe Campaign of 1944-45, because of geography, climate and a tactical situation more akin to the trench warfare of 1914-18. It had nevertheless placed a premium on the same qualities as previous wars; professional and tactical skills, the endurance of extremes of temperature, the capacity to make-do and by self-help to enjoy some tolerable degree of comfort, and strict attention to duty.

In lighter vein, the things most often remembered by those who served in Korea were the acquisition of jeeps and .50 calibre machine-guns from the United States Army in exchange for Scotch Whisky, the string vests and 'long johns' (undergarments of winter clothing), and the ham and lima beans of US Army 'C' Rations. Particularly when out of the line, all ranks had enjoyed excellent rations including turkeys and steaks issued on a scale per man appropriate to the appetite of Australian jackaroos in the outback. Another vital morale factor was that letters took an average of only five days from the posting box at home to their issue by the Orderly Sergeant in squadron camps. Rumour had it that SSM Gilliland rationed 'C' Squadron Leader to one letter a day in order to reduce the incidence of Major Walker's 'ink-storms' even if one delivery brought a batch of letters to him

## THE FINAL DAYS

from Denmark. Officers from 'C' Squadron out shooting pheasants accidentally peppered a South Korean laundering his smalls while the 'B' Betting Book records that 'Major Tomkin and Lieutenant Fane jointly lay Second Lieutenant Barnes £15 to £5 that he would not, on the move of 'B' into the lines on 19th April 1952, get the four tanks of his troop to their positions on Hill 355 without the assistance of the Squadron or other fitters. Alas, Mr Barnes lost his bet.

On top of the world.
Lieutenant 'Mike' Fane on Hill 132.

# Last Thoughts
(Major General Henry Woods)

The motto of the "Skins" - "Vestigia Nulla Retrorsum" (The Rest Never Retreat) – is very apposite to this Anthology and to the compilation thereof. It is a record of events sixty years ago before the universal influence of television, motorways or the arrival of children who now approach retirement. His late majesty, George V1, died that year and both he and The Queen have shown us the example of real devotion to duty and the truth in the words of our Regimental Collect –
"No man having put his hand to the plough and looking back is fit for Thy Kingdom".

My reflections over a lifetime of Service in and for the regiment convince me that those experiences on active service have not changed in the 326 years of our parent Regiments' existence. This year their successors in the ranks of the The Royal Dragoon Guards will endure the same stress of long hours, tiredness, irregular meals and the enemy threats, as well as separation from loved ones, which faced those who fought at Dettingen, Waterloo in the Crimea or Normandy. Weather conditions and terrain also play their part, however sophisticated the modern technologies and weaponry may be. Some parallels may be drawn between and the operations in Northern Ireland, Iraq and Afghanistan, and each may help to raise professional expertise and standards. The Korean War has no operational lessons of value today. The only points which may link past and present members of the Regiment more closely are:-

The extraordinary spirit and comradeship within the 1st Commonwealth Division and its component units.

UN operations undertaken with the full authority of the United Nations Security Council.

# LAST THOUGHTS

We can claim to have played a part in achieving the truce which has subsisted in Korea for more than half a century. At least so far a renewal of war has not taken place and though our role tended to be static and at times boring, we all knew the value of our contribution.

Some paid with their lives; we honour their memory and it is to them and to all who served with us that this Anthology is dedicated.

## CASUALTIES
### AS AT NOVEMBER 5th, 1952
#### Wounded.

Captain P. A. Duckworth.
Captain I. G. Manning.
Captain P. K. Cuthbert.
Lieut. W. F. A. Findlay.
Lieut. D. P. Rowat.
2/Lt. A. C. B. Critchley-Waring.
2/Lt. F. C. Sutherland.
Sgt. J. Love.
Sgt. A. McCreadie.
Sgt. D. Osborne.
Cpl. E. Burdass.
Cpl. T. Reynolds.
Cpl. A. Booth.
L/Cpl. D. Raymond.
Tpr. L. Ford.
Tpr. A. Goodwin.
Tpr. G. Lucas.
Tpr. W. Simpson.
Tpr. R. Bottrell.
Tpr. S. Brown.
Tpr. B. Goman.
Tpr. D. Thorpe.
Tpr. J. Holman.
Tpr. D. McLelland.
Cfn. T. Cummins.
Cfn. J. McMillan.
Cfn. J. Hulley.

# HONOURS AND AWARDS – KOREA 1952

MBE    Major HC Walker
        Major GT Blundell-Brown
        Regimental Quartermaster Sergeant Green
MC     Captain CE Taylor
        Captain GS Murray (8th KRIH 1951)
        Lieutenant MJC Anstice
MM    Sergeant Irving
BEM   Squadron Sergeant Major Gilliland

**Mentioned in Dispatches**
Lieutenant Colonel R de C Vigors
Captain GL Wathen
Lieutenant (QM) F Birchall
Squadron Sergeant Major J Clayton
Squadron Sergeant Major C Gower
Squadron Quartermaster Sergeant P Musk
Sergeant F Cowling
Sergeant S Hubbard

**Commander-in-Chief's Certificates**
Lieutenant DP Rowat
Lieutenant GMG Swindells
Squadron Quartermaster Sergeant CJ Boardman
Sergeant R Bleach
Sergeant D Whetmore
Sergeant J Gibson, ACC Attached
Staff Sergeant J Myers, REME Attached
Corporal R Newport
Sergeant R Shellam, RAMC Attached
Trooper N Hedges

## HONOURS AND AWARDS

## 235 British Korean Veterans

In 1950, 22 States of the United Nations (UN) joined South Korean forces to repel the North Korean aggression and stop the spread of Communism. During the three years of the conflict some four million people died. Over 100,000 British Servicemen served during the war of whom over 2,000 were killed or taken prisoner. Among many decorations awarded were four Victoria Crosses.

In 1952 the Commonwealth units from Australia, Canada, India, New Zealand and South Africa combined to form the 1st Commonwealth Division.

The Memorial Garden, originally laid out and maintained by members of the British Korean Veterans Association (BKVA), is designed to create a living Memorial to all British Servicemen who served and gave their lives. It is an arboretum within an arboretum planted with more than 100 trees of some 23 different species mostly of Korean or Asian origin.

TRACKS IN KOREA

## ROLL OF HONOUR

SGMN. R. LATHAM (R. SIGS) JANUARY 1952
TPR. D. R. VEASEY 26TH JANUARY 1952
CPL. R. BREWER 20TH MAY 1952
2ND LIEUT. A.J. ALBRECHT 20TH JANUARY 1952
CPL. R. STEGGLES 12TH JULY 1952
TPR. J. P. CAHILL 4TH JANUARY 1952
TPR. P. MCFADYEN 4TH SEPTEMBER 1952
CPL. G. B. COOK (RNZAC) 4TH SEPTEMBER 1952
L/CPL D. METCALF 4TH SEPTEMBER 1952
SGT. N. E. WYKES 4TH SEPTEMBER 1952
TPR. J. W. GRACE 5TH NOVEMBER 1952
CPL. B. O. SMITH 15TH NOVEMBER 1952

"For Your Tomorrow We Gave Our Today."

212

# ABSENT VETERANS
by David Lidstone,
Private The Royal Gloucester Regiment

Would that you could wander still,
Through grassy fields, by wooded hill
When morning bird-song fills the air
And yet another spring is here.

If only you could still feel the sun
Upon your face when winter's done
And smell sweet-scented flowers fair
When yet another summer's here.

But fate decided otherwise
And you, beneath Korean skies,
A gallant band of comrades lie,
Your duty done, your merit high.

No changing seasons can erase
That once familiar name, that face
Which comes and lingers in each thought
Of those with whom we lived and fought

# TRACKS IN KOREA

The President of the Republic of Korea

June 1, 2010

A Letter of Thanks

This year as we commemorate the sixtieth anniversary of the outbreak of the Korean War, we honor your selfless sacrifice in fighting tyranny and aggression. We salute your courage in enduring the unimaginable horrors of war. We pay tribute to your commitment in protecting liberty and freedom.

We Koreans made a promise to build a strong and prosperous country that upholds peace and freedom so that the sacrifices that you made would not have been in vain. We have faithfully kept that promise. Korea today is a vibrant democracy with a robust economy and we are actively promoting peace and stability around the world. Korea transformed itself from a country of received aid to one that provides aid to others. We are proud of what we managed to accomplish and we wish to dedicate these achievements to you.

The Korean government has been inviting Korean War veterans every year as part of its Revisit Korea Program since 1975. This year we will be inviting 2,400 Korean War veterans and their families. We Koreans and myself in particular look forward to welcoming you. We hope that you will see what you made possible and hope that your families will feel renewed pride in what you did for us many years ago.

Please accept, once again, our warmest gratitude and deepest respect. You will always remain our true Heroes and we assure you that we will continue to do our best to make you proud. On behalf of the Korean people, I would like to say "Thank you."

Sincerely yours,

Lee Myung-bak
President, Republic of Korea